DATE DUE		
AUG. 3 1 1988		
FE 1 5 '88		
AP 23 '90		
AG 5 '91		
JUN 06 '95		
JL 29 98		
OC 30 08		

821.008
N   5899

Norman, Charles, 1904–   *ed.*
    Come live with me; five centuries of romantic poetry.
With an introd. and notes. New York, McKay ₁1966₎

    xxvi, 294 p. 21 cm.

EAU CLAIRE DISTRICT LIBRARY

    1. Love poetry. 2. English poetry (Collections) 3. American
poetry (Collections)   I. Title.

PR1184.N6   821.0083   66–17074

Library of Congress   ₁5₎

Come Live with Me

BY CHARLES NORMAN

SELECTED POEMS

❧ ❧

THE MUSES' DARLING: CHRISTOPHER MARLOWE
SO WORTHY A FRIEND: WILLIAM SHAKESPEARE
MR. ODDITY: SAMUEL JOHNSON, LL.D.
E. E. CUMMINGS
EZRA POUND
THE PLAYMAKER OF AVON

❧ ❧

POETS ON POETRY

Come Live with Me

Five Centuries of Romantic Poetry

With an Introduction
and Notes by *******

Charles Norman

DAVID McKAY COMPANY, INC. • NEW YORK

COME LIVE WITH ME

COPYRIGHT © 1966 BY CHARLES NORMAN

LIBRARY OF CONGRESS CATALOG CARD NUMBER: 66–17074

MANUFACTURED IN THE UNITED STATES OF AMERICA

ACKNOWLEDGMENTS

The editor thanks Cambridge University Press for permission to use four poems from *Rare Poems of the Seventeenth Century* chosen and edited by L. Birkett Marshall.

"Feather," "Lakes" and "A Cry" by Francesco Bianco copyright 1957 by Fairleigh Dickinson University (*The Literary Review*) ; copyright © 1966 by Francesco M. Bianco. "Washington Square" by Francesco Bianco copyright © 1966 by Francesco M. Bianco. "A Cry" and "Washington Square" © 1966 by *Art and Literature,* SELA (Société Anonyme d'Editions Littéraires et Artistiques).

"Catherine Takes a Stroll" and "A Valentine" from *With Hey Ho . . . and The Man With the Spats* by John Cournos copyright © 1963 by Astra Books; copyright 1965 by John Cournos.

"All in green went my love riding" copyright 1923, 1951 by E. E. Cummings. Reprinted from his volume *Poems 1923–1954* by permission of Harcourt, Brace & World, Inc. "Puella Mea" copyright 1923, 1951 by E. E. Cummings. Reprinted from *Poems 1923–1954* by permission of Harcourt, Brace & World, Inc. "Tumbling hair" copyright 1923, 1951 by E. E. Cummings. Reprinted from *Poems 1923–1954* by permission of Harcourt, Brace & World, Inc. "Paris: this April sunset completely utters" copyright 1925 by E. E. Cummings. Reprinted from *Poems 1923–1954* by permission of Harcourt, Brace & World, Inc. "cruelly, love" copyright 1925 by E. E. Cummings. Reprinted from *Poems 1923–1954* by permission of Harcourt, Brace & World, Inc.

"Alas" and "The Ghost" by Walter de la Mare used by permission of The Literary Trustees of Walter de la Mare and The Society of Authors as their representative.

"The Dead Poet" by Lord Alfred Douglas used by permission of Martin Secker & Warburg Ltd.

"La Figlia Che Piange" from *Collected Poems 1909–1962* by T. S. Eliot, copyright 1936 by Harcourt, Brace & World, Inc.; copyright © 1963, 1964 by T. S. Eliot. Reprinted by permission of Harcourt, Brace & World, Inc., and Faber & Faber Ltd.

"The Telephone" and "My November Guest" from *Complete Poems of Robert Frost.* Copyright 1916, 1934 by Holt, Rinehart and Winston, Inc. Copyright 1944, © 1962 by Robert Frost. Reprinted by permission of Holt, Rinehart and Winston, Inc.

"Pied Beauty" from *Poems of Gerard Manley Hopkins,* Third Edition, edited by W. H. Gardner. Copyright 1948 by Oxford University Press, Inc. Reprinted by permission.

"Reveille," "Bredon Hill," "Along the field as we came by," "On Wenlock Edge" and "Oh see how thick the goldcup flowers" from *A Shropshire Lad—* Authorized Edition—from *The Collected Poems of A. E. Housman.* Copyright

1939, 1940, © 1959 by Holt, Rinehart and Winston, Inc. Reprinted by permission of Holt, Rinehart and Winston, Inc. Permission granted by The Society of Authors as the literary representative of the Estate of the late A. E. Housman, and Messrs. Jonathan Cape Ltd., publishers of A. E. Housman's *Collected Poems.*
"The chestnut casts his flambeaux" from *The Collected Poems of A. E. Housman.* Copyright 1922 by Holt, Rinehart and Winston, Inc. Copyright 1950 by Barclays Bank Ltd. Reprinted by permission of Holt, Rinehart and Winston, Inc. Permission granted by The Society of Authors as the literary representative of the Estate of the late A. E. Housman, and Messrs. Jonathan Cape Ltd., publishers of A. E. Housman's *Collected Poems.*
"Strings in the earth and air" from *The Collected Poems of James Joyce.* Copyright 1918 by B. W. Huebsch, Inc., 1946 by Nora Joyce. Reprinted by permission of The Viking Press, Inc.
"The Bridegroom," a section from "Epitaphs of the War," copyright 1919 by Rudyard Kipling; reprinted from *Rudyard Kipling's Verse: Definitive Edition* by permission of Mrs. George Bambridge and Doubleday & Co., Inc., and The Macmillan Company of Canada.
"The Wife of Llew" from *The Complete Poems of Francis Ledwidge* published by Brentano's, 1919; reprinted by permission of Coward-McCann, Inc.
"Come, live with me and be my love," from *A Time to Dance,* copyright 1933, 1961 by C. Day Lewis; reprinted by permission of The Harold Matson Co., Inc., and Jonathan Cape Ltd.
"Envoi (1919)" and "Portrait d'Une Femme" by Ezra Pound from *Personae,* copyright 1926, 1954 by Ezra Pound. Reprinted by permission of the publisher, New Directions.
"Another Dark Lady" reprinted with permission of The Macmillan Company from *Collected Poems* by E. A. Robinson. Copyright 1916 by E. A. Robinson. Copyright renewed 1944 by Ruth Nivison. "Miniver Cheevy" (copyright 1907 by Charles Scribner's Sons; renewal copyright 1935) is reprinted with the permission of Charles Scribner's Sons from *The Town Down the River* by Edwin Arlington Robinson.
"Polite Song" from *The Paradox in the Circle* by Theodore Spencer copyright 1941 by New Directions. Reprinted by permission of the publisher, New Directions.
"Peter Quince at the Clavier" and "Two Figures in Dense Violet Light" copyright 1923 by Wallace Stevens. Renewed 1951. Reprinted with permission of Alfred A. Knopf, Inc., from *The Collected Poems of Wallace Stevens.*
"In My Craft or Sullen Art" from *The Collected Poems of Dylan Thomas* copyright 1939, 1942, 1946, © 1957 by New Directions. Copyright 1952, 1953 by Dylan Thomas. Reprinted by permission of the publisher, New Directions.
"Adlestrop" from *Collected Poems* by Edward Thomas, Faber & Faber Ltd., publishers, reprinted by permission of Mrs. Helen Thomas.
"Pastoral" and "October" by Willard Trask copyright 1958 by Fairleigh Dickinson University (*The Literary Review*); copyright © 1966 by Willard Trask.
"Romance" from *The Dark Wind* by W. J. Turner copyright 1920 by E. P. Dutton & Co., Inc. Renewal 1948 by Mrs. Delphine Turner. Reprinted by permission of the publishers.

"Sunday Evening in the Common" is reprinted with the permission of Charles Scribner's Sons from *Poems Old and New* by John Hall Wheelock.

"Saint Apollinare in Classe" from *The Holy Wells of Orris* by R. N. D. Wilson is reprinted with the permission of The Bodley Head Ltd.

"The Song of Wandering Aengus" and "He Thinks Of Those Who Have Spoken Evil of His Beloved" reprinted with permission of The Macmillan Company from *Poems* by William Butler Yeats. Copyright 1906 by The Macmillan Company. Copyright renewed 1934 by William B. Yeats. "A Woman Homer Sung," "A Drinking Song" and "The Mask" reprinted with permission of The Macmillan Company from *The Green Helmet and Other Poems* by William Butler Yeats. Copyright 1912 by The Macmillan Company. Copyright renewed 1940 by Bertha Georgie Yeats. "Brown Penny" reprinted with permission of The Macmillan Company from *The Collected Poems of W. B. Yeats*. Copyright 1912 by The Macmillan Company. Copyright renewed 1940 by Bertha Georgie Yeats. "Politics" reprinted with permission of The Macmillan Company from *Last Poems and Plays* by William Butler Yeats. Copyright 1940 by Georgie Yeats. Permission to reprint these poems from *The Collected Poems of W. B. Yeats* granted by Mr. M. B. Yeats and The Macmillan Company of Canada.

To

THE MEMORY OF A GENTLEWOMAN

M. C. B.

Contents

2. POETRY AND MUSIC

3. THE FABLED WORLD

4. HOMAGE TO SHAKESPEARE

5. 'COME LIVE WITH ME . . . '

6. A SHROPSHIRE MEDLEY

7. LOVE

8. LOVERS

9. LADIES

10. PEOPLE

12. SEASONS

Introduction

It is now more than fifty years since T. S. Eliot wrote the first of those poems that are uniquely modern and that ushered in a new period, with Ezra Pound its godfather and guide.* That period appears to have come to an end. In the course of wearing itself out it has become blurred by a species of writing which is, in the main, a correspondence with the world, and like much correspondence, intermittently a diary and travelogue.

But poetry is not really a form of communication—it is a transfer of experience from the poet to the reader. There are other aspects: a poem is not merely the culmination and record of a poet's experience—it is itself a new experience. And to endure, it must have in it the quality described by Allen Tate in the essay entitled "Tension in Poetry," which serves our time much as Matthew Arnold's "The Study of Poetry" served his— the quality, that is to say, of lines that have finality.

There is yet another characteristic of enduring work: it is entirely itself, belonging unquestionably to its own time, but is seen to have an affinity with works that have preceded it, and will prove to have an affinity with works of the future. All poets belong to the same generation. The collection that follows is an attempt to demonstrate this. It is offered in the belief that a new movement in literature, based on the wellsprings of English and a return to form, is about to be, or is being, ushered in. It may turn out to be a romantic movement.

Arnold wrote: "In poetry, which is thought and art in one, it is the glory, the eternal honor, that charlatanism shall find no en-

* "The Love Song of J. Alfred Prufrock," 1911; published four years later through Pound's efforts.

trance; that this noble sphere be kept inviolate and inviolable. Charlatanism is for confusing or obliterating the distinctions between excellent and inferior, sound and unsound or only half-sound, true or untrue or only half-true." He also stated the case for reading: "There can be no more useful help for discovering what poetry belongs to the class of the truly excellent, and can therefore do us most good, than to have always in one's mind lines and expressions of the great masters, and to apply them as a touch-stone to other poetry."

Anthologies tend to fall into two main categories: the chronological, or historical; and the personal. The present collection is personal; in it, continuity and influence take the place of mere chronology. For while each of the poems chosen can stand alone, some will be found enhanced by their proximity to poems inspired by them in whole or in part. The idea for Poe's "Annabel Lee" will be seen in a stanza by the Duke of Buckinghamshire, Pound's "Envoi (1919)" in a brace of poems by Edmund Waller, "Tumbling-hair" by E. E. Cummings in a passage of Milton's "Paradise Lost." For a seventeenth-century view of Donne's most famous lyric, it has been paired with the reply to it by William Habington.

"Homage to Shakespeare" brings together, I believe for the first time, the poems addressed to him by his contemporaries, while a whole section has been devoted to the poems inspired by Marlowe's "Come live with me," beginning with two lyrics—from the Provençal and Spanish—which may have been the source of that best-known Elizabethan poem.

Several translations and adaptations from Latin poets whose influence was pervasive have been included, together with some poems familiar to old readers, though not necessarily to new ones. But this is not the place to tell what lies in store; the text reveals it, and the notes after each section give such information as the editor possessed that he deemed useful or entertaining. One observation may be made: the subjects in this book—poets and poetry; the real and fabled world; love, lovers, and ladies—are all seen through the eyes of men.

CHARLES NORMAN

1.

Poets and Poetry

1. POETS AND POETRY

TO HIS BOOK

Go, little book: thyself present
As child whose parent is unkent,
To him that is the president
Of noblesse and of chivalry,
And if that envy bark at thee,
As sure it will, for succor flee
    Under the shadow of his wing;
And askèd, who thee forth did bring,
A shepherd's swain say did thee sing,
All as his straying flock he fed;
And when his honor has thee read,
Crave pardon for my hardihead.
    But if that any ask thy name,
Say thou wert base begot with blame,
For-thy thereof thou takest shame.
And when thou art past jeopardy,
Come tell me what was said of me,
And I will send more after thee.

EDMUND SPENSER

Book: *The Shepherd's Calendar,*
   published anonymously
unkent: unknown
president: Sir Philip Sidney
For-thy: therefore

3

HE THINKS OF THOSE WHO HAVE
SPOKEN EVIL OF HIS BELOVED

Half close your eyelids, loosen your hair,
And dream about the great and their pride;
They have spoken against you everywhere,
But weigh this song with the great and their pride;
I made it out of a mouthful of air,
Their children's children shall say they have lied.

WILLIAM BUTLER YEATS

FEATHER

Time consumes each word:
time, and poor usage, and a negligent style;
but the Poet invests with grace
noble and base alike, and he gives weight to a feather.

Every word reveals to him its sweetness,
as does a woman to her lover in close joy,
who trembles, and smiles, and whispers, 'Ah, never,
for you my youth, my youth must never die.'

Ravished, he notes; and one day, if the Dark
Muse demands it, remembering all, he recalls
those sounds to life; and in an airy frame
of flowers, and marbles, heartbeats and green boughs,

Builds he a garden paradisial,
shining in never-ending spring;
but in that garden none but the desperate may enter—
none but he who has drunk, Dionysius! thy wine.

Ah, why did I not know these things
in my mad April days, my mad, my fleeting April,
which I wasted wandering without rest,
and exiled from the laurel and the rose?

Now that I am become slow at the fierce game of love,
and I lack the poet's craft,
I cannot tell which it is—more cruel,
or more useless—the fire that burns me up.

But steadfast against all hazards, good or bad,
you, Poet, stand! outlasting the long years;
and you smile to the sorry pupil, who is searching for you,
with wet eyes, in the Anthology;

And you call him, you invite him to that garden,
which he glimpsed once, and hardly hopes to enter.
Let your spring blossom for him, too—
let happiness sing to him in your language.

FRANCESCO BIANCO

⚞ ⚟

PAST RUIN'D ILION HELEN LIVES

Past ruin'd Ilion Helen lives,
   Alcestis rises from the shades;
Verse calls them forth; 'tis verse that gives
   Immortal youth to mortal maids.

Soon shall Oblivion's deepening veil
   Hide all the peopled hills you see,
The gay, the proud, while lovers hail
   These many summers you and me.

WALTER SAVAGE LANDOR

Ilion: Troy
Alcestis: who died that her husband might live

WHEN I HAVE FEARS THAT
I MAY CEASE TO BE

When I have fears that I may cease to be
   Before my pen has glean'd my teeming brain,
Before high-pilèd books, in charact'ry,
   Hold like rich garners the full-ripen'd grain;
When I behold, upon the night's starr'd face,
   Huge cloudy symbols of a high romance,
And think that I may never live to trace
   Their shadows, with the magic hand of chance;
And when I feel, fair creature of an hour!
   That I shall never look upon thee more,
Never have relish in the faery power
   Of unreflecting love!—then on the shore
Of the wide world I stand alone, and think
Till love and fame to nothingness do sink.

JOHN KEATS

THE MOTTO

Tentanda via est, &c.

What shall I do to be forever known,
   And make the age to come my own?
I shall like beasts or common people die,
   Unless you write my elegy.
Whilst others great by being born are grown,
   Their mothers' labor, not their own,

In this scale gold, in th' other fame does lie;
    The weight of that mounts this so high.
These men are Fortune's jewels, moulded bright,
    Brought forth with their own fire and light;
If I, her vulgar stone, for either look,
    Out of myself it must be strook.
Yet I must on; what sound is't strikes mine ear?
    Sure I Fame's trumpet hear;
It sounds like the last trumpet, for it can
    Raise up the buried man.
Unpast Alps stop me, but I'll cut through all,
    And march, the Muses' Hannibal.
Hence all the flattering vanities that lay
    Nets of roses in the way;
Hence the desire of honors or estate,
    And all that is not above Fate.
Hence Love himself, that tyrant of my days,
    Which intercepts my coming praise.
Come, my best friends, my books, and lead me on,
    'Tis time that I were gone;
Welcome, great Stagirite, and teach me now
    All I was born to know;
Thy scholar's victories thou dost far outdo—
    He conquered th' earth, the whole world you.
Welcome, learned Cicero, whose blest tongue and wit
    Preserves Rome's greatness yet;
Thou art the first of orators—only he
    Who best can praise thee next must be.
Welcome, the Mantuan Swan, Virgil the wise,
    Whose verse walks highest, but not flies,
Who brought green poesy to her perfect age,
    And made that art which was a rage.
Tell me, ye mighty three, what shall I do
    To be like one of you?
But you have climbed the mountain's top, there sit
    On the calm, flourishing head of it,

And whilst with wearied steps we upward go,
  See us, and clouds, below.

ABRAHAM COWLEY

Tentanda via est: A way must be found to raise myself
  from earth and hover on men's lips triumphantly (Virgil,
  Georgics, III)
Stagirite: Aristotle, a native of Stageira
Thy scholar's victories: Alexander the Great's

≫ ≪

AFTER HORACE: SONNET LV

Not marble, nor the gilded monuments
Of princes, shall outlive this powerful rime;
But you shall shine more bright in these contents
Than unswept stone, besmear'd with sluttish time.
When wasteful war shall statues overturn,
And broils root out the work of masonry,
Nor Mars his sword nor war's quick fire shall burn
The living record of your memory.
'Gainst death and all-oblivious enmity
Shall you pace forth; your praise shall still find room
Even in the eyes of all posterity
That wear this world out to the ending doom.
  So, till the judgment that yourself arise,
  You live in this, and dwell in lovers' eyes.

WILLIAM SHAKESPEARE

broils: tumults

OVID, BOOK I, ELEGY 15

Envy, why carpest thou my time is spent so ill,
And term'st my works fruits of an idle quill,
Or that unlike the line from whence I sprung
War's dusty honors are refused, being young,
Nor that I study not the brawling laws,
Nor set my voice to sale in every cause?
Thy scope is mortal, mine eternal fame,
That all the world may ever chant my name.
Homer shall live while Tenedos stands, and Ide,
Or into sea swift Simoïs doth slide;
Ascraeus lives while grapes with new wine swell,
Or men with crooked sickles corn down fell;
The world shall of Callimachus ever speak—
His art excelled, although his wit was weak;
Forever lasts high Sophocles' proud vein;
With sun and moon Aratus shall remain;
While bondsmen cheat, fathers [are] hard, bawds whorish,
And strumpets flatter, shall Menander flourish;
Rude Ennius, and Plautus full of wit,
Are both in Fame's eternal legend writ;
What age of Varro's name shall not be told,
And Jason's Argo and the fleece of gold?
Lofty Lucretïus shall live that hour
That Nature shall dissolve this earthly bower;
Aeneas' war, and Tityrus, shall be read
While Rome of all the conquered world is head;
Till Cupid's bow and fiery shafts be broken,
Thy verses, sweet Tibullus, shall be spoken;
And Gallus shall be known from east to west,
So shall Licoris, whom he lovèd best.
Therefore, when flint and iron wear away,
Verse is immortal and shall ne'er decay;
To verse let kings give place, and kingly shows,
And banks o'er which gold-bearing Tagus flows.

Let base conceited wits admire vile things—
Fair Phoebus lead me to the Muses' springs;
About my head be quivering myrtle wound,
And in sad lovers' heads let me be found;
The living, not the dead, can envy bite,
For after death all men receive their right;
Then, though death rakes my bones in funeral fire,
I'll live, and as he pulls me down, mount higher.

                                   CHRISTOPHER MARLOWE

NOT LOVE, NOT WAR . . .

Not love, not war, nor the tumultuous swell
Of civil conflict, nor the wrecks of change,
Nor duty struggling with afflictions strange—
Not these alone inspire the tuneful shell;
But where untroubled peace and concord dwell,
There also is the Muse not loath to range,
Watching the twilight smoke of cot or grange,
Skyward ascending from a woody dell.
Meek aspirations please her, lone endeavor,
And sage content, and placid melancholy;
She loves to gaze upon a crystal river—
Diaphanous because it travels slowly;
Soft is the music that would charm forever;
The flower of sweetest smell is shy and lowly.

                                   WILLIAM WORDSWORTH

THE COMPLAINT OF CHAUCER
TO HIS PURSE

To you, my purse, and to none other wight,
Complain I, for ye be my lady dear!
I am so sorry, now that ye been light,
For certes, but ye make me heavy cheer;
Me were as lief be laid upon my bier.
For which unto your mercy thus I cry:
Beëth heavy again, or else might I die!

Now voucheth safe this day, or it be night,
That I of you the blissful sound may hear,
Or see your color like the sun—bright—
That of yellowness had never peer;
Ye be my life, ye be mine heart's steer.
Queen of comfort and of good company:
Beëth heavy again, or else might I die!

Now, purse, that been to me my life's light
And savior—as down in this world here—
Out of this town help me through your might,
Since that ye will not be my treasurer;
For I am shaved as nigh as any frere.
But yet I pray unto your courtesy:
Beëth heavy again, or else might I die!

L'ENVOY

O conqueror of Brutus' Albion,
Which that by line and free electïon
Been very king, this song to you I send;
And ye, that mighten all our harms amend,
Have mind upon my supplicatïon!

GEOFFREY CHAUCER

CHAUCER

An old man in a lodge within a park;
The chamber walls depicted all around
With portraitures of huntsman, hawk, and hound,
And the hurt deer. He listeneth to the lark,
Whose song comes with the sunshine through the dark
Of painted glass in leaden lattice bound;
He listeneth and he laugheth at the sound,
Then writeth in a book like any clerk.
He is the poet of the dawn, who wrote
The *Canterbury Tales,* and his old age
Made beautiful with song; and as I read
I hear the crowing cock, I hear the note
Of lark and linnet, and from every page
Rise odors of ploughed field or flowery mead.

HENRY WADSWORTH LONGFELLOW

Chaucer 1.
wight: person
steer: rudder
down: fleece or feathers
here: (not redundant) probably "at this time"
shaved as nigh as any frere: tonsured like a friar
conqueror of Brutus' Albion: Brutus was tradi-
    tionally thought to have founded Britain. The
    "Complaint" was addressed to the recently
    crowned Henry IV, who renewed an old and
    gave Chaucer a new grant, plus a hogshead of
    wine

Chaucer 2.
clerk: pronounced "clark"—a cleric or scholar

THE HONOR DONE TO POETS OF OLD
AND MODERN POETS

Past ages did the ancient poets grace,
And to their swelling styles the very place
Where they were born denomination lent;
Publius Ovidius Naso had th' ostent
Of Sulmonensis added, and did give
The dorp a name by which it still doth live.
Publius Virgilius likewise had th' addition
Of Maro to express his full condition.
Marcus Annaeus Lucanus Seneca,
Bore title from his city Cordova.
Caius Pedo was styl'd Albinovanus,
Aurelius Olympius, Nemesianus.
   Some from the nature of their poems: thus,
Caius Lucilius was call'd Satyrus;
So Livius Andronicus, Epicus;
And Lucius Accius surnamed Tragicus.
Some from their several countries, because they
Were foreign-born: Terence, from Africa,
Is Publius Terentius Afer read,
Titus Calpurnius, Siculus, as bred
In Sicily. So many others had
(And that for sundry causes) means to add
Unto their first, for with their worth increast
Their styles: the most grac'd with three names at least.
   Our modern poets to that pass are driven,
Those names are curtail'd which they first had given,
And, as we wisht to have their memories drown'd,
We scarcely can afford them half their sound.
   Greene, who had in both academies ta'en
Degree of Master, yet could never gain
To be call'd more than Robin; who, had he
Profess'd ought save the Muse, serv'd, and been free
After a seven years' prenticeship, might have

(With credit, too) gone Robert to his grave.
Marlowe, renown'd for his rare art and wit,
Could ne'er attain beyond the name of Kit,
Although his *Hero and Leander* did
Merit addition rather. Famous Kyd
Was call'd but Tom. Tom Watson, though he wrote
Able to make Apollo's self to dote
Upon his Muse, for all that he could strive,
Yet never could to his full name arrive.
Tom Nashe (in his time of no small esteem)
Could not a second syllable redeem.
Excellent Beaumont, in the foremost rank
Of the rar'st wits, was never more than Frank.
Mellifluous Shakespeare, whose enchanting quill
Commanded mirth or passion, was but Will.
And famous Jonson, though his learnèd pen
Be dipp'd in Castalay, is still but Ben.
Fletcher and Webster, of that learnèd pack
None of the mean'st, yet neither was but Jack.
Decker's but Tom, and May, and Middleton;
And he's now but Jack Ford that once was John.

 Nor speak I this that any here exprest
Should think themselves less worthy than the rest,
Whose names have their full syllable and sound;
Or that Frank, Kit or Jack are the least wound
Unto their fame and merit. I, for my part,
(Think others what they please) accept that heart
Which courts my love in most familiar phrase,
And that it takes not from my pains or praise.
If anyone to me so bluntly come,
I hold he loves me best that calls me Tom.

THOMAS HEYWOOD

styles: titles, names
dorp: Ovidiopol, near Odessa, Ukrainian S.S.R., once identi-
 fied with the site of Tomi, where Ovid spent his exile.
 But now it is believed to be Constanta, formerly Tomi,

THOMAS HEYWOOD

Tom, if they loved thee best who called thee Tom,
   What else may all men call thee, seeing thus bright
   Even yet the laughing and the weeping light
That still thy kind old eyes are kindled from?
Small care was thine to assail and overcome
   Time and his child Oblivion: yet of right
   Thy name has part with names of lordlier might
For English love and homely sense of home,
Whose fragrance keeps thy small sweet bayleaf young
   And gives it place aloft among thy peers
     Whence many a wreath once higher strong Time has hurled:
And this thy praise is sweet on Shakespeare's tongue—
   'O good old man, how well in thee appears
     The constant service of the antique world!'

ALGERNON CHARLES SWINBURNE

bayleaf: from the wreath signifying heroic or poetic fame

O good old man! how well in thee appears
The constant service of the antique world,
When service sweat for duty, not for meed!
Thou art not for the fashion of these times—
Orlando to Adam, in *As You Like It,*
   Act II, Scene 3.
   Swinburne's sonnet to Heywood is one of
   a cycle entitled "Dramatic Poets"

---

     on the Black Sea
   both academies: Oxford and Cambridge
   Hero and Leander: left a fragment, continued by George
     Chapman
   Castalay: fount of poesy

THE EPISTLE DEDICATORY
TO THE ILIADS OF HOMER, PRINCE OF POETS

To the High-Born Prince of Men, Henry; Thrice Royal Inheritor
to the United Kingdoms of Great Britain, etc.

Since perfect happiness, by princes sought,
Is not with birth born, nor exchequers bought;
Nor follows in great trains; nor is possessed
With any outward state; but makes him blest
That governs inward; and beholdeth there
All his affections stand about him bare;
That by his power can send to Tower and death
All traitorous passions, marshaling beneath
His justice his mere will; and in his mind
Holds such a sceptre, as can keep confined
His whole life's actions in the royal bounds
Of virtue and religion; and their grounds
Takes in to sow his honors, his delights,
And complete empire; you should learn these rights
(Great prince of men) by princely precedents;
Which here, in all kinds, my true zeal presents
To furnish your youth's groundwork, and first state;
And let you see one godlike man create
All sorts of worthiest men; to be contrived
In your worth only; giving him revived,
For whose life Alexander would have given
One of his kingdoms; who (as sent from heaven,
And thinking well, that so divine a creature
Would never more enrich the race of nature)
Kept as his crown his works, and thought them still
His angels, in all power to rule his will;
And would affirm that Homer's poesy
Did more advance his Asian victory,
Than all his armies. Oh! 'tis wondrous much

(Though nothing prized) that the right virtuous touch
Of a well-written soul to virtue moves.
Nor have we souls to purpose, if their loves
Of fitting objects be not so inflamed.
How much, then, were this kingdom's main soul maimed,
To want this great inflamer of all powers
That move in human souls? All realms but yours
Are honored with him, and hold blest that state
That have his works to read and contemplate:
In which, humanity to her height is raised,
Which all the world (yet, none enough) hath praised.
Seas, earth, and heaven, he did in verse comprise,
Outsung the Muses, and did equalize
Their king Apollo; being so far from cause
Of princes' light thoughts, that their gravest laws
May find stuff to be fashioned by his lines.
Through all the pomp of kingdoms still he shines,
And graceth all his gracers. Then let lie
Your lutes, and viols, and more loftily
Make the heroics of your Homer sung;
To drums and trumpets set his angel's tongue,
And, with the princely sport of hawks you use,
Behold the kingly flight of his high Muse,
And see how, like the phoenix, she renews
Her age and starry feathers in your sun;
Thousands of years attending, every one
Blowing the holy fire, and throwing in
Their seasons, kingdoms, nations, that have been
Subverted in them: laws, religions, all
Offered to change and greedy funeral;
Yet still your Homer lasting, living, reigning,
And proves, how firm truth builds in poets' feigning.

GEORGE CHAPMAN

Homer's poesy, etc.: Alexander the Great carried Homer's work
  into battle

ON FIRST LOOKING INTO
CHAPMAN'S HOMER

Much have I travelled in the realms of gold,
    And many goodly states and kingdoms seen;
    Round many western islands have I been
Which bards in fealty to Apollo hold.
Oft of one wide expanse had I been told
    That deep-brow'd Homer ruled as his demesne:
    Yet did I never breathe its pure serene
Till I heard Chapman speak out loud and bold:
Then felt I like some watcher of the skies
    When a new planet swims into his ken;
Or like stout Cortez, when with eagle eyes
    He stared at the Pacific—and all his men
Looked at each other with a wild surmise—
    Silent, upon a peak in Darien.

JOHN KEATS

❧ ❦

MEMORABILIA

Ah, did you once see Shelley plain,
    And did he stop and speak to you,
And did you speak to him again?
    How strange it seems and new!

But you were living before that,
    And also you are living after;
And the memory I started at—
    My starting moves your laughter!

I crossed a moor, with a name of its own
    And a certain use in the world no doubt,
Yet a hand's-breadth of it shines alone
    'Mid the blank miles round about.

For there I picked up on the heather,
    And there I put inside my breast
A moulted feather, an eagle-feather!
    Well, I forget the rest.

ROBERT BROWNING

THE DEAD POET

I dreamed of him last night, I saw his face
All radiant and unshadowed of distress,
And as of old, in music measureless,
I heard his golden voice and marked him trace
Under the common thing the hidden grace,
And conjure wonder out of emptiness,
Till mean things put on beauty like a dress
And all the world was an enchanted place.

And then methought outside a fast locked gate
I mourned the loss of unrecorded words,
Forgotten tales and mysteries half said,
Wonders that might have been articulate,
And voiceless thoughts like murdered singing birds.
And so I woke and knew that he was dead.

LORD ALFRED DOUGLAS

The Dead Poet: Oscar Wilde

ALONE

From childhood's hour I have not been
As others were—I have not seen
As others saw—I could not bring
My passions from a common spring.
From the same source I have not taken
My sorrow; I could not awaken
My heart to joy at the same tone;
And all I lov'd, *I* lov'd alone.
Then—in my childhood—in the dawn
Of a most stormy life—was drawn
From ev'ry depth of good and ill
The mystery which binds me still:
From the torrent, or the fountain,
From the red cliff of the mountain,
From the sun that 'round me roll'd
In its autumn tint of gold—
From the lightning in the sky
As it pass'd me flying by—
From the thunder and the storm,
And the cloud that took the form
(When the rest of Heaven was blue)
Of a demon in my view.

EDGAR ALLAN POE

AUSTERITY OF POETRY

That son of Italy who tried to blow,
Ere Dante came, the trump of sacred song,
In his light youth amid a festal throng
Sate with his bride to see a public show.
Fair was the bride, and on her front did glow
Youth like a star; and what to youth belong—
Gay raiment, sparkling gauds, elation strong.

A prop gave way! crash fell a platform! lo,
'Mid struggling sufferers, hurt to death, she lay!
Shuddering, they drew her garments off—and found
A robe of sackcloth next the smooth, white skin.
Such, poets, is your bride, the Muse! young, gay,
Radiant, adorn'd outside; a hidden ground
Of thought and of austerity within.

MATTHEW ARNOLD

That son of Italy: Jacopone da Todi

IN MY CRAFT OR SULLEN ART

In my craft or sullen art
Exercised in the still night
When only the moon rages
And the lovers lie abed
With all their griefs in their arms,
I labor by singing light
Not for ambition or bread
Or the strut and trade of charms
On the ivory stages
But for the common wages
Of their most secret heart.

Not for the proud man apart
From the raging moon I write
On these spindrift pages
Nor for the towering dead
With their nightingales and psalms
But for the lovers, their arms
Round the griefs of the ages,
Who pay no praise or wages
Nor heed my craft or art.

DYLAN THOMAS

➣ *NOTES* ➣

The Shepherd's Calendar, 1579, was dedicated "To the Noble and Virtuous Gentleman most worthy of all titles both of learning and chivalry M[aster]. Philip Sidney." Spenser's poem, "To His Book," given here with his name, was originally signed "Immerito." But every poet knows his own worth, and Spenser was no exception, as shown by Sonnet LXXV of the *Amoretti:*

> One day I wrote her name upon the strand,
> But came the waves and washèd it away;
> Again I wrote it with a second hand,
> But came the tide, and made my pains his prey.
> 'Vain man,' said she, 'that dost in vain essay
> A mortal thing so to immortalize,
> For I myself shall like to this decay,
> And eke my name be wipèd out likewise.'
> 'Not so,' quoth I; 'let baser things devise
> To die in dust, but you shall live in fame;
> My verse your virtues rare shall eternize,
> And in the heavens write your glorious name,
> Where, whenas death shall all the world subdue,
> Our love shall live, and later life renew.'

The experience and the boast were repeated by Landor in "Ianthe's Name":

> Well I remember how you smiled
>   To see me write your name upon
> The soft sea-sand . . . *'O! what a child!*
>   *You think you're writing upon stone!'*
> I have since written what no tide
>   Shall ever wash away, what men
> Unborn shall read o'er ocean wide
>   And find Ianthe's name again.

His poem in the preceding section was also addressed to "Ianthe," in real life, Mrs. Sophia Jane Swift, whom Landor knew for forty years. Though otherwise irascible enough, he had a genius for friendship with young ladies (see his poem in Section 6, and notes).

Francesco Bianco was born in Turin, Italy, but died an American citizen (for dates, see Index of Poets). His wife was Margery Williams

Bianco, the well-known writer of children's books. Their daughter, Pamela Bianco, the painter, won fame at the age of twelve with an exhibition of drawings at the Leicester Galleries, London; Walter de la Mare wrote a series of poems to "illustrate" those drawings, and their joint effort appeared as a book entitled *Flora.* Bianco left twenty-nine poems, many of which—including those in this book—he translated himself. (For a fuller account of the man and his work, see the present editor's "To the Memory of Francesco Bianco," *The Literary Review,* Vol. I, No. 1, 1957.) This is his first appearance in book form. For a poem from *Flora,* see "Alas," Section 3.

Of Abraham Cowley, Dr. Johnson wrote in his *Lives of the Poets:* "In the window of his mother's apartment lay Spenser's *Fairy Queen;* in which he very early took delight to read, till by feeling the charms of verse, he became, as he relates, irrecoverably a poet." Sir John Denham, who wrote Cowley's elegy, gave him this incomparable praise:

> To him no author was unknown,
> Yet what he wrote was all his own.

The first two lines of Shakespeare's sonnet are a literal translation from Horace, Book III, Ode 30; he also drew from the poem by Ovid, given here in the translation by Marlowe.

C. F. Tucker Brooke, the great editor of Marlowe's *Works* (Oxford, 1910), preferred Ben Jonson's version of Elegy 15, which follows Marlowe's in the surreptitiously printed *All Ovid's Elegies* (there is no date on the earliest title pages; copies of one edition were publicly burned on June 4, 1599, by order of the Archbishop of Canterbury and the Bishop of London). Earlier editors—Gifford, Dyce—believed both versions were by Jonson; Professor Brooke thought that Jonson "filed and polished Marlowe's crude version before inserting it as his own into the *Poetaster.*" I prefer Marlowe's, but have taken one word from Jonson —"sprung," at the end of the third line; Marlowe had "come." It is from this elegy that Shakespeare took his motto for *Venus and Adonis:*

> Vilia miretur vulgus; mihi flavus Apollo
> Pocula Castalia plena ministret aqua
>
> Let base conceited wits admire vile things—
> Fair Phoebus lead me to the Muses' springs.

Printed with the *Elegies* were forty-eight epigrams by J. D. (Sir John Davies) ; to judge by their contents, the wrath of the churchmen was probably directed against these; but see "Ovid, Book I, Elegy 5," in Section 8.

Thomas Heywood was one of the most prolific authors of a prolific age—really two ages—and outlived most of his Elizabethan and Jacobean fellow poets and playwrights. The roll call of their names (and those of another golden age) occurs in Book 4 of *The Hierarchie of the blessed Angells,* 1635. Davies has an epigram about him:

> *In Heywoodum.* 29.
> Heywood, that did in epigrams excel,
> Is now put down since my light Muse arose,
> As Buckets are put down into a well,
> Or as a school boy putteth down his hose

(*i.e.,* breeches, to be whipped). Michael Drayton also wrote a rhymed recollection of poets he had known, with the title, "To my most dearly-beloved friend, Henry Reynolds, Esquire, of Poets and Poetry," first published in 1627. It is, in general, dull, but contains this praise of Marlowe:

> Marlowe, bathèd in the Thespian springs,
> Had in him those brave translunary things
> That the first poets had; his raptures were
> All air and fire, which made his verses clear,
> For that fine madness still he did retain
> Which rightly should possess a poet's brain.

The praise of Shakespeare is tepid by comparison:

> And be it said of thee,
> Shakespeare, thou hadst as smooth a comic vein,
> Fitting the sock, and in thy natural brain
> As strong conception and as clear a rage
> As anyone that trafficked with the stage.

sock: from *soccus,* comic actor's shoe

2.

Poetry and Music

2. POETRY AND MUSIC

ENVOI (1919)

Go, dumb-born book,
Tell her that sang me once that song of Lawes:
Hadst thou but song
As thou hast subjects known,
Then were there cause in thee that should condone
Even my faults that heavy upon me lie,
And build her glories their longevity.

Tell her that sheds
Such treasure in the air,
Recking naught else but that her graces give
Life to the moment,
I would bid them live
As roses might, in magic amber laid,
Red overwrought with orange and all made
One substance and one color
Braving time.

Tell her that goes
With song upon her lips
But sings not out the song, nor knows
The maker of it, some other mouth,
May be as fair as hers,
Might, in new ages, gain her worshippers,
When our two dusts with Waller's shall be laid,

Siftings on siftings in oblivion,
Till change hath broken down
All things save Beauty alone.

EZRA POUND

TO MR. HENRY LAWES

who had then newly set a song of mine in the year 1635

Verse makes heroic virtue live;
But you can life to verses give.
As when in open air we blow,
And breath, though strain'd, sounds flat and low;
But if a trumpet take the blast,
It lifts it high, and makes it last:
So in your airs our numbers dress'd,
Make a shrill sally from the breast
Of nymphs, who, singing what we penn'd,
Our passions to themselves commend;
While love, victorious with thy art,
Governs at once their voice and heart.

You by the help of tune and time,
Can make that song that was but rhyme.
Noy pleading, no man doubts the cause;
Or questions verses set by Lawes.

As a church window, thick with paint,
Lets in a light but dim and faint;
So others, with division, hide
The light of sense, the poet's pride:
But you alone may proudly boast
That not a syllable is lost;
The writer's, and the setter's skill
At once the ravish'd ears do fill.
Let those which only warble long,
And gargle in their throats a song,

Content themselves with Ut, Re, Mi:
Let words, and sense, be set by thee.

Noy pleading: William Noy, or Noye,
  Attorney General, 1631–1634—
  hence pun in following line

SONG

Go lovely Rose,
Tell her that wastes her time and me,
  That now she knows
When I resemble her to thee,
  How sweet and fair she seems to be.

Tell her that's young,
And shuns to have her graces spied,
  That hadst thou sprung
In deserts, where no men abide,
  Thou must have uncommended died.

Small is the worth
Of Beauty from the light retir'd;
  Bid her come forth,
Suffer her self to be desir'd,
  And not blush so to be admir'd.

Then die, that she,
The common fate of all things rare,
  May read in thee
How small a part of time they share,
  That are so wondrous sweet and fair.

EDMUND WALLER

TO HIS FRIEND MASTER R. L.,

In Praise of Music and Poetry

If music and sweet poetry agree,
As they must needs, the sister and the brother,

Then must the love be great 'twixt thee and me,
Because thou lov'st the one, and I the other.
Dowland to thee is dear, whose heavenly touch
Upon the lute doth ravish human sense;
Spenser, to me, whose deep conceit is such
As, passing all conceit, needs no defense.
Thou lov'st to hear the sweet melodious sound
That Phoebus' lute, the queen of music, makes;
And I in deep delight am chiefly drowned
Whenas himself to singing he betakes:
    One god is god of both, as poets feign;
    One knight loves both, and both in thee remain.

RICHARD BARNFIELD

conceit: fancy

ON THE PRAISE OF POETRY [*AND MUSIC*]

'Tis not a pyramid of marble stone,
    Though high as our ambitïon;
'Tis not a tomb cut out in brass, which can
    Give life to th' ashes of a man,
But verses only. They shall fresh appear
    Whilst there are men to read or hear,
When time shall make the lasting brass decay
    And eat the pyramid away,
Turning that monument wherein men trust
    Their names to what it keeps, poor dust;
Then shall the epitaph remain, and be
    New graven in eternity.
Poets by death are conquered, but the wit
    Of poets triumphs over it.

What cannot verse? When Thracian Orpheus took
    His lyre, and gently on it strook,
The learnèd stones came dancing all along,
    And kept time to the charming song.
With artificial pace the warlike pine,
    The elm and his wife, the ivy twine,
With all the better trees, which erst had stood
    Unmoved, forsook their native wood.
The laurel to the poet's hand did bow,
    Craving the honor of his brow;
And every loving arm embraced and made
    With their officious leaves a shade.
The beasts, too, strove his auditors to be,
    Forgetting their old tyranny;
The fearful hart next to the lion came,
    And wolf was shepherd to the lamb;
Nightingales, harmless sirens of the air,
    And muses of the place, were there,
Who when their little windpipes they had found
    Unequal to so strange a sound,
O'ercome by art and grief they did expire,
    And fell upon the conquering lyre—
Happy, O happy they, whose tomb might be,
    Mausolus, envièd by thee!

ABRAHAM COWLEY

Mausolus: King of Caria, whose widow erected a magnificent tomb (whence mausoleum)

≥ ≤

MUSIC'S DUEL

Now westward Sol had spent the richest beams
Of noon's high glory, when hard by the streams
Of Tiber, on the scene of a green plat,
Under protection of an oak, there sat

A sweet lute-master, in whose gentle airs
He lost the day's heat and his own hot cares.

    Close in the covert of the leaves there stood
A nightingale, come from the neighboring wood
(The sweet inhabitant of each glad tree,
Their muse, their siren; harmless siren she).
There stood she list'ning, and did entertain
The music's soft report and mould the same
In her own murmurs, that whatever mood
His curious fingers lent, her voice made good.
The man perceiv'd his rival and her art,
Dispos'd to give the lightfoot lady sport,
Awakes his lute, and 'gainst the fight to come,
Informs it in a sweet Preludium
Of closer strains, and ere the war begin,
He lightly skirmishes on every string,
Charg'd with a flying touch; and straightway she
Carves out her dainty voice as readily
Into a thousand sweet distinguish'd tones,
And reckons up in soft divisïons
Quick volumes of wild notes to let him know,
By that shrill taste, she could do something, too.

    His nimble hands' instinct then taught each string
A cap'ring cheerfulness and made them sing
To their own dance; now negligently rash
He throws his arm, and with a long drawn dash
Blends all together; then distinctly trips
From this to that; then quick returning skips,
And snatches this again, and pauses there.
She measures every measure, everywhere
Meets art with art; sometimes, as if in doubt,
Not perfect yet, and fearing to be out
Trails her plain ditty in one long-spun note
Through the sleek passage of her open throat,
A clear, unwrinkled song; then doth she point it

With tender accents and severely joint it
By short diminutives, that being rear'd
In controverting warbles evenly shar'd,
With her sweet self she wrangles. He, amazed
That from so small a channel should be rais'd
The torrent of a voice whose melody
Could melt into such sweet variety,
Strains higher yet, that tickled with rare art
The tatling strings (each breathing in his part)
Most kindly do fall out: the grumbling bass
In surly groans disdains the treble's grace;
The high-perch'd treble chirps at this, and chides,
Until his finger (Moderator) hides
And closes the sweet quarrel, rousing all—
Hoarse, shrill, at once—as when the trumpets call
Hot Mars to th' harvest of death's field, and woo
Men's hearts into their hands. This lesson, too,
She gives him back; her supple breast thrills out
Sharp airs, and staggers in a warbling doubt
Of dallying sweetness, hovers o'er her skill,
And folds in wav'd notes with a trembling bill
The pliant series of her slippery song;
Then starts she suddenly into a throng
Of short, thick sobs whose thund'ring volleys float
And roll themselves over her lubric throat
In panting murmurs, still'd out of her breast
That ever-bubbling spring, the sugar'd nest
Of her delicious soul that there does lie
Bathing in streams of liquid melody,
Music's best seed-plot, whence in ripen'd airs
A golden-headed harvest fairly rears
His honey-dropping tops, plough'd by her breath,
Which there reciprocally laboureth
In that sweet soil. It seems a holy choir
Founded to th' name of great Apollo's lyre,
Whose silver roof rings with the sprightly notes
Of sweet-lipp'd angel-imps, that swill their throats

In cream of morning Helicon, and then
Prefer soft anthems to the ears of men
To woo them from their beds, still murmuring
That men can sleep while they their matins sing
(Most divine service) whose so early lay
Prevents the eyelids of the blushing day.
There might you hear her kindle her soft voice,
In the close murmur of a sparkling noise,
And lay the groundwork of her hopeful song,
Still keeping in the forward stream so long,
Till a sweet whirlwind (striving to get out)
Heaves her soft bosom, wanders round about,
And makes a pretty earthquake in her breast,
Till the fledg'd notes at length forsake their nest,
Fluttering in wanton shoals, and to the sky,
Wing'd with their own wild echo's pratling, fly.
She opes the floodgate, and lets loose a tide
Of streaming sweetness which in state doth ride
On the wav'd back of every swelling strain,
Rising and falling in a pompous train;
And while she thus discharges a shrill peal
Of flashing airs, she qualifies their zeal
With the cool epode of a graver note,
Thus high, thus low, as if her silver throat
Would reach the brazen voice of war's hoarse bird;
Her little soul is ravish'd, and so pour'd
Into loose ectasies, that she is plac't
Above herself, Music's enthusiast.

Shame now, and anger, mix'd a double stain
In the musician's face; yet once again
(Mistress) I come. Now reach a strain, my lute,
Above her mock, or be forever mute;
Or tune a song of victory to me,
Or thyself sing thine own obsequy.
So said, his hands sprightly as fire he flings,
And with a quavering coyness tests the strings;

The sweet-lipp'd sisters musically frighted,
Singing their fears are fearfully delighted,
Trembling as when Apollo's golden hairs
Are fann'd and frizzl'd in the wanton airs
Of his own breath which, married to his lyre,
Doth tune the spheres and make heaven's self look higher.
From this to that, from that to this he flies,
Feels music's pulse in all her arteries;
Caught in a net which there Apollo spreads,
His fingers struggle with the vocal threads;
Following those little rills, he sinks into
A sea of Helicon; his hand does go
Those parts of sweetness which with nectar drop,
Softer than that which pants in Hebe's cup.
The humorous strings expound his learnèd touch
By various glosses: now they seem to grutch,
And murmur in a buzzing din, then gingle
In shrill-tongu'd accents, striving to be single;
Every smooth turn, every delicious stroke,
Gives life to some new grace; thus doth he invoke
Sweetness by all her names; thus, bravely thus
(Fraught with a fury so harmonious)
The lute's light genius now does proudly rise,
Heav'd on the surges of swollen rhapsodies,
Whose flourish (meteor-like) doth curl the air
With flash of high-born fancies; here and there
Dancing in lofty measures, and anon
Creeps on the soft touch of a tender tone
Whose trembling murmurs, melting in wild airs,
Run to and fro, complaining his sweet cares
Because those precious mysteries that dwell
In music's ravish'd soul he dare not tell,
But whisper to the world. Thus do they vary
Each string his note, as if they meant to carry
Their master's blest soul (snatch'd out at his ears
By a strong ecstasy) through all the spheres
Of Music's heaven, and seat it there on high

In the empyrean of pure harmony.
At length (after so long, so loud a strife
Of all the strings, still breathing the best life
Of blest variety attending on
His fingers' fairest revolutïon
In many a sweet rise, many as sweet a fall)
A full-mouth diapason swallows all.

    This done, he lists what she would say to this,
And she, although her breath's late exercise
Had dealt too roughly with her tender throat,
Yet summons all her sweet powers for a note—
Alas! in vain! For while (sweet soul) she tries
To measure all those wild diversities
Of chatt'ring strings by the small size of one
Poor simple voice, rais'd in a natural tone,
She fails, and failing grieves, and grieving dies.
She dies; and leaves her life the victor's prize,
Falling upon his lute. O fit to have
(That liv'd so sweetly) dead so sweet a grave!

RICHARD CRASHAW

still'd: distilled
Helicon: mountain sacred to Muses
prefer: submit
war's hoarse bird: the raven
obsequy: funeral rite

ON LUTESTRINGS CAT-EATEN

    Are these the strings that poets feign
Have cleared the air and calmed the main,
Charmed wolves, and from the mountain crests
Made forests dance with all their beasts?
Could these neglected shreds you see
Inspire a lute of ivory

And make it speak? Oh! think then what
Hath been committed by my cat,
Who, in the silence of this night,
Hath gnawn these cords and marred them quite,
Leaving such relics as may be
For frets, not for my lute, but me.
Puss, I will curse thee: may'st thou dwell
With some dry hermit in a cell
Where rat ne'er peeped, where mouse ne'er fed,
And flies go supperless to bed;
Or with some close-pared brother, where
Thou'lt fast each sabbath in the year;
Or else, profane, be hanged on Monday
For butchering a mouse on Sunday.
Or may'st thou tumble from some tower,
And miss to light upon all four,
Taking a fall that may untie
Eight of nine lives and let them fly;
Or may the midnight embers singe
Thy dainty coat, or Jane beswinge
Thy hide, when she shall take thee biting
Her cheese clouts, or her house beshiting.
What, was there ne'er a rat nor mouse,
Nor buttery ope? nought in the house
But harmless lutestrings could suffice
Thy paunch and draw thy glaring eyes?
Did not thy conscious stomach find
Nature profaned, that kind with kind
Should stanch his hunger? think on that,
Thou cannibal and Cyclops cat.
For know, thou wretch, that every string
Is a cat-gut which art doth spin
Into a thread; and how suppose
Dunstan, that snuffed the devil's nose,
Should bid these strings revive, as once
He did the calf from naked bones;
Or I, to plague thee for thy sin,

Should draw a circle, and begin
To conjure, for I am, look to't,
An Oxford scholar and can do't;
Then with three sets of maps and mows,
Seven of odd words, and motley shows,
A thousand tricks, that may be taken
From Faustus, Lamb, or Friar Bacon,
I should begin to call my strings
My catlings and my minikins,
And they, recallèd, straight should fall
To mew, to purr, to caterwaul
From puss's belly. Sure as death,
Puss should be an engastrimyth;
Puss should be sent for to the king
For a strange bird or some rare thing;
Puss should be sought to far and near
As she some cunning woman were;
Puss should be carried up and down,
From shire to shire, from town to town,
Like to the camel, lean as hag,
The elephant or apish egg,
For a strange sight; puss should be sung
In lousy ballads midst the throng
At markets, with as good a grace
As 'Agincourt' or 'Chevy Chase';
The Troy-sprung Briton would forgo
His pedigree he chanteth so,
And sing that Merlin, long deceast,
Returned is in a nine-lived beast.
    Thus, puss, thou seest what might betide thee,
But I forbear to hurt or chide thee;
For maybe puss was melancholy,
And so to make her blithe and jolly,
Finding these strings, she'ld have a fit
Of mirth; nay, puss, if that were it,
Thus I revenge me, that as thou
Hast played on them, I've played on you,

And as thy touch was nothing fine,
So I've but scratched these notes of mine.

THOMAS MASTERS

engastrimyth: ventriloquist
cunning woman: witch

❧ ❦

THE COMMENDATION OF MUSIC

When whispering strains, with creeping wind,
   Distil soft passion through the heart;
And when at every touch we find
    Our pulses beat and bear a part;
      When threads can make
      A heart-string shake,
      Philosophy
      Can not deny
   Our souls consist of harmony.

When unto heavenly joys, we feign
   Whate'er the soul affecteth most,
Which only thus we can explain,
    By music of the heavenly host,
      Whose lays, methinks,
      Makes stars to shrink,
      Philosophy
      May judge thereby
   Our souls consist of harmony.

Oh, lull me, lull me, charming air!
   My senses rock with wonder sweet;
Like snow on wool thy fallings are,
    Soft as a spirit's are thy feet;
      Grief who need fear
      That hath an ear?

Down let him lie
And slumbering die,
And change his soul for harmony.

WILLIAM STRODE

❧ ❦

FOLLOW YOUR SAINT, FOLLOW WITH ACCENTS SWEET

Follow your saint, follow with accents sweet;
Haste you, sad notes, fall at her flying feet.
There, wrapped in cloud of sorrow, pity move,
And tell the ravisher of my soul I perish for her love.
But if she scorns my never-ceasing pain,
Then burst with sighing in her sight and ne'er return again.

All that I sung still to her praise did tend,
Still she was first, still she my songs did end.
Yet she my love and music both doth fly,
The music that her echo is and beauty's sympathy.
Then let my notes pursue her scornful flight:
It shall suffice that they were breathed and died for her delight.

THOMAS CAMPION

A DRINKING SONG

Wine comes in at the mouth
And love comes in at the eye;
That's all we shall know for truth
Before we grow old and die.
I lift the glass to my mouth,
I look at you, and I sigh.

WILLIAM BUTLER YEATS

CELIA SINGING

You that think Love can convey
    No other way
But through the eyes, into the heart,
    His fatal dart,
Close up those casements, and but hear
    This siren sing;
    And on the wing
Of her sweet voice, it shall appear
That Love can enter at the ear.

THOMAS CAREW

GRATIANA DANCING AND SINGING

See! with what constant motïon,
Even and glorious as the sun,
    Gratiana steers that noble frame,
Soft as her breast, sweet as her voice
That gave each winding law and poise,
    And swifter than the wings of Fame.

She beat the happy pavëment
By such a star made firmament,
    Which now no more the roof envìes;
But swells up high, with Atlas even,
Bearing the brighter, nobler heaven,
    And, in her, all the deities.

Each step trod out a lover's thought
And the ambitious hopes he brought,
   Chained to her brave feet with such arts,
Such sweet command and gentle awe,
As, when she ceased, we sighing saw
   The floor lay paved with broken hearts.

So did she move; so did she sing,
Like the harmonious spheres that bring
   Unto their rounds their music's aid;
Which she performèd such a way
As all the enamored world will say,
   'The Graces danced, and Apollo played.'

RICHARD LOVELACE

⤐ ⤏

THE REMOTE BERMUDAS

ARIEL'S SONG

Come unto these yellow sands,
   And then take hands:
Curtsied when you have, and kiss'd,—
   The wild waves whist,—
Foot it featly here and there;
And, sweet sprites, the burden bear.
   Hark, hark!
       Bow, wow,
   The watch-dogs bark:
       Bow, wow.
   Hark, hark! I hear
The strain of strutting Chanticleer,
       Cock-a-diddle-dow.

FERDINAND

Where should this music be? i' th' air, or th' earth?
It sounds no more;—and sure, it waits upon
Some god o' th' island. Sitting on a bank,
Weeping again the king my father's wrack,
This music crept by me upon the waters,
Allaying both their fury, and my passion,
With its sweet air: thence I have follow'd it,—
Or it hath drawn me rather,—but 'tis gone.
No, it begins again.

ARIEL *Sings*

Full fathom five thy father lies;
  Of his bones are coral made;
Those are pearls that were his eyes:
  Nothing of him that doth fade,
But doth suffer a sea-change
Into something rich and strange.
Sea-nymphs hourly ring his knell:
                Ding, dong.
  Hark! now I hear them,—
                Ding-dong, bell.

WILLIAM SHAKESPEARE

PETER QUINCE AT THE CLAVIER

I

Just as my fingers on these keys
Make music, so the selfsame sounds
On my spirit make a music, too.

Music is feeling, then, not sound;
And thus it is that what I feel,
Here in this room, desiring you,

Thinking of your blue-shadowed silk,
Is music. It is like the strain
Waked in the elders by Susanna.

Of a green evening, clear and warm,
She bathed in her still garden, while
The red-eyed elders watching, felt

The basses of their beings throb
In witching chords, and their thin blood
Pulse pizzicati of Hosanna.

II

In the green water, clear and warm,
Susanna lay.
She searched
The touch of springs,
And found
Concealed imaginings.
She sighed,
For so much melody.

Upon the bank, she stood
In the cool
Of spent emotions.
She felt, among the leaves,
The dew
Of old devotions.

She walked upon the grass,
Still quavering.
The winds were like her maids,
On timid feet,
Fetching her woven scarves,
Yet wavering.

A breath upon her hand
Muted the night.
She turned—

A cymbal crashed,
And roaring horns.

III

Soon, with a noise like tambourines,
Came her attendant Byzantines.

They wondered why Susanna cried
Against the elders by her side;

And as they whispered, the refrain
Was like a willow swept by rain.

Anon, their lamps' uplifted flame
Revealed Susanna and her shame.

And then, the simpering Byzantines
Fled, with a noise like tambourines.

IV

Beauty is momentary in the mind—
The fitful tracing of a portal;
But in the flesh it is immortal.
The body dies; the body's beauty lives.
So evenings die, in their green going,
A wave, interminably flowing.
So gardens die, their meek breath scenting
The cowl of winter, done repenting.
So maidens die, to the auroral
Celebration of a maiden's choral.
Susanna's music touched the bawdy strings
Of those white elders; but, escaping,
Left only Death's ironic scraping.
Now, in its immortality, it plays
On the clear viol of her memory,
And makes a constant sacrament of praise.

WALLACE STEVENS

STRINGS IN THE EARTH AND AIR

Strings in the earth and air
 Make music sweet;
Strings by the river where
 The willows meet.

There's music along the river
 For Love wanders there,
Pale flowers on his mantle,
 Dark leaves on his hair.

All softly playing,
 With head to the music bent,
And fingers straying
 Upon an instrument.

JAMES JOYCE

⪦ *NOTES* ⪧

Pound has been very secretive about who sang him Waller's "Song" in the setting by Lawes. And there I must leave it. Milton, like Waller, wrote a poem addressed "To Mr. H. Lawes, on his Airs." But what is probably his most exquisite praise of music occurs at the end of "L'Allegro":

> And ever against eating cares,
> Lap me in soft Lydian airs,
> Married to immortal verse;
> Such as the meeting soul may pierce
> In notes, with many a winding bout
> Of linkèd sweetness long drawn out,
> With wanton heed, and giddy cunning,
> The melting voice through mazes running,
> Untwisting all the chains that tie
> The hidden soul of harmony.

The passage has curious resemblances to some parts of "Music's Duel," given in the text, adapted by Crashaw from a Latin poem by Famianus Strada (1572–1649) and paraphrased as well by John Ford; William Strode, author of "The Commendation of Music" in this section; and Ambrose Phillips.

Thomas Masters was an Oxford scholar and divine. He wrote poems in English, Latin, and Greek; but no book by him is known. His "On Lutestrings Cat-Eaten" is from a British Museum manuscript, Harley MS. 6917 (see *Rare Poems of the Seventeenth Century,* chosen and edited by L. Birkett Marshall, Cambridge University Press, 1936; p. 157).

Campion's "Follow Your Saint," for which a musical setting seems superfluous, appeared in P. Rosseter's *A Book of Airs,* 1601. Thereafter he published four *Books of Airs* of his own, both words and music. He is also the author of *Observations in the Art of English Poetry.*

"Ariel's Song," etc., is from *The Tempest,* Act I, Scene 2. Shakespeare's interest in music finds expression in all the plays, and in the *Sonnets* as well. It is even possible to follow the trail of his Dark Lady

by finding those sonnets in which physical images appear, as in this
one (CXXVIII) where she is at the virginal:

> How oft, when thou, my music, music play'st,
> Upon that blessed wood whose motion sounds
> With thy sweet fingers, when thou gently sway'st
> The wiry concord that mine ear confounds,
> Do I envy those jacks that nimble leap
> To kiss the tender inward of thy hand,
> Whilst my poor lips, which should that harvest reap,
> At the wood's boldness by thee blushing stand!
> To be so tickl'd, they would change their state
> And situation with those dancing chips,
> O'er whom thy fingers walk with gentle gait,
> Making dead wood more bless'd than living lips.
>   Since saucy jacks so happy are in this,
>   Give them thy fingers, me thy lips to kiss.

3.

The Fabled World

3. THE FABLED WORLD

TUMBLING-HAIR

Tumbling-hair
        picker of buttercups
                violets
dandelions
And the big bullying daisies
                through the field wonderful
with eyes a little sorry
Another comes
        also picking flowers

E. E. CUMMINGS

SONG

With fair Ceres, Queen of Grain,
  The reapèd fields we roam;
Each country peasant, nymph, and swain,
  Sing their harvest home;
Whilst the Queen of Plenty hallows
Growing fields as well as fallows.

THOMAS HEYWOOD

fallows: uncultivated ground

ADAM AND EVE

The birds their choir apply; airs, vernal airs,
Breathing the smell of field and grove, attune
The trembling leaves, while universal Pan,
Knit with the Graces and the Hours in dance,
Led on the eternal Spring. Not that fair field
Of Enna, where Proserpine gathering flowers,
Herself a fairer flower, by gloomy Dis
Was gather'd, which cost Ceres all that pain
To seek her through the world; nor that sweet grove
Of Daphne by Orontes, and the inspired
Castalian spring, might with this Paradise
Of Eden strive; nor that Nyseian isle
Girt with the river Triton, where old Cham,
Whom Gentiles Ammon call and Libyan Jove,
Hid Amalthea, and her florid son
Young Bacchus, from his stepdame Rhea's eye;
Nor where Abassin kings their issue guard,
Mount Amara, though this by some supposed
True Paradise, under the Ethiop line
By Nilus' head, enclosed with shining rock,
A whole day's journey high, but wide remote
From this Assyrian garden, where the fiend
Saw, undelighted, all delight, all kind
Of living creatures, new to sight and strange.
Two of far nobler shape, erect and tall,
Godlike erect, with native honor clad,
In naked majesty seem'd lords of all,
And worthy seem'd: for in their looks divine
The image of their glorious Maker shone,
Truth, wisdom, sanctitude severe and pure
(Severe, but in true filial freedom placed),
Whence true authority in men; though both
Not equal, as their sex not equal seem'd:
For contemplation he and valor form'd;
For softness she, and sweet attractive grace;

He for God only, she for God in him.
His fair large front and eye sublime declared
Absolute rule; and hyacinthine locks
Round from his parted forelock manly hung
Clustering, but not beneath his shoulders broad;
She, as a veil, down to the slender waist
Her unadornèd golden tresses wore
Dishevell'd, but in wanton ringlets waved,
As the vine curls her tendrils, which implied
Subjection, but required with gentle sway,
And by her yielded, by him best received,
Yielded with coy submission, modest pride,
And sweet, reluctant, amorous delay.
Nor those mysterious parts were then conceal'd;
Then was not guilty shame—dishonest shame
Of nature's works, honor dishonorable,
Sin-bred, how have ye troubled all mankind
With shows instead, mere shows of seeming pure,
And banish'd from man's life his happiest life,
Simplicity and spotless innocence!
So pass'd they naked on, nor shunn'd the sight
Of God or angel, for they thought no ill;
So hand in hand they pass'd, the loveliest pair
That ever since in love's embraces met—
Adam, the goodliest man of men since born
His sons, the fairest of her daughters Eve.
Under a tuft of shade that on a green
Stood whispering soft, by a fresh fountain-side
They sat them down; and, after no more toil
Of their sweet gardening labor than sufficed
To recommend cool zephyr, and made ease
More easy, wholesome thirst and appetite
More grateful, to their supper-fruits they fell,
Nectarine fruits, which the compliant boughs
Yielded them, sidelong as they sat reclined
On the soft downy bank damask'd with flowers;
The savory pulp they chew, and in the rind

Still as they thirsted scoop the brimming stream;
Nor gentle purpose, nor endearing smiles
Wanted, nor youthful dalliance as beseems
Fair couple, link'd in happy mutual league,
Alone as they. About them frisking play'd
All beasts of th' earth, since wild, and of all chase
In wood or wilderness, forest or den;
Sporting the lion ramp'd, and in his paw
Dandled the kid; bears, tigers, ounces, pards,
Gambol'd before them; th' unwieldy elephant,
To make them mirth, used all his might, and wreath'd
His lithe proboscis; close the serpent sly
Insinuating, wove with Gordian twine
His braided train, and of his fatal guile
Gave proof unheeded; others on the grass
Couch'd, and now fill'd with pasture gazing sat,
Or bedward ruminating, for the sun,
Declin'd, was hasting now with prone career
To th' ocean isles, and in th' ascending scale
Of heaven the stars that usher evening rose;
When Satan, still in gaze, as first he stood,
Scarce thus at length fail'd speech recover'd sad.

SATAN

Creatures of other mould, earth-born perhaps,
Not spirits, yet to heav'nly spirits bright
Little inferior; whom my thoughts pursue
With wonder, and could love, so lively shines
In them divine resemblance, and such grace
The hand that form'd them on their shape hath pour'd.
Ah, gentle pair, ye little think how nigh
Your change approaches, when all these delights
Will vanish and deliver ye to woe,
More woe, the more your taste is now of joy.

ADAM

Sole partner and sole part of all these joys,
Dearer thyself than all, needs must the Power
That made us, and for us this ample world,
Be infinitely good, and of his good
As liberal, and free as infinite.

EVE

                    O thou for whom
And from whom I was form'd, flesh of thy flesh,
And without whom am to no end, my guide
And head, what thou hast said is just and right;
For we to him indeed all praises owe
And daily thanks—I, chiefly, who enjoy
So far the happier lot, enjoying thee.

SATAN

Sight hateful, sight tormenting! thus these two,
Emparadis'd in one another's arms,
The happier Eden, shall enjoy their fill
Of bliss on bliss, while I to Hell am thrust,
Where neither joy nor love, but fierce desire,
Among our other torments not the least,
Still unfulfill'd with pain of longing pines.

ADAM

                    Fair Consort, th' hour
Of night, and all things now retir'd to rest,
Mind us of like repose.

EVE

With thee conversing, I forget all time,
All seasons and their change, all please alike.
Sweet is the breath of morn, her rising sweet,
With charm of earliest birds; pleasant the sun

When first on this delightful land he spreads
His orient beams, on herb, tree, fruit, and flower,
Glist'ring with dew; fragrant the fertile earth
After soft showers; and sweet the coming on
Of grateful evening mild, then silent night
With this her solemn bird and this fair moon,
And these, the gems of heaven, her starry train;
But neither breath of morn when she ascends
With charm of earliest birds, nor rising sun
On this delightful land, nor herb, fruit, flower,
Glist'ring with dew, nor fragrance after showers,
Nor grateful evening mild, nor silent night
With this her solemn bird, nor walk by moon,
Or glittering starlight, without thee is sweet.

JOHN MILTON

Dis: Pluto, king of the underworld
Ceres: goddess of earth and mother of **Proserpine**
the fiend: Satan, looking for mischief
ounce: lynx
pard: leopard

TO HELEN

Helen, thy beauty is to me
    Like those Nicean barks of yore,
That gently, o'er a perfumed sea,
    The weary, way-worn wanderer bore
    To his own native shore.

On desperate seas long wont to roam,
    Thy hyacinth hair, thy classic face,
Thy Naiad airs have brought me home
    To the glory that was Greece
And the grandeur that was Rome.

Lo! in yon brilliant window-niche
    How statue-like I see thee stand!

The agate lamp within thy hand,
Ah! Psyche, from the regions which
Are Holy Land!

EDGAR ALLAN POE

THE WIFE OF LLEW

And Gwydion said to Math, when it was spring:
'Come now and let us make a wife for Llew.'
And so they broke broad boughs yet moist with dew,
And in a shadow made a magic ring:
They took the violet and the meadow-sweet
To form her pretty face, and for her feet
They built a mound of daisies on a wing,
And for her voice they made a linnet sing
In the wide poppy blowing for her mouth.
And over all they chanted twenty hours.
And Llew came singing from the azure south
And bore away his wife of birds and flowers.

FRANCIS LEDWIDGE

VENUS AND ADONIS

Venus, by Adonis' side,
Crying kissed, and kissing cried,
Wrung her hands and tore her hair
For Adonis dying there.

'Stay!' quoth she, 'Oh, stay and live!
Nature surely doth not give
To the earth her sweetest flowers,
To be seen but some few hours.'

On his face, still as he bled,
For each drop, a tear she shed,
Which she kissed or wiped away,
Else had drowned him where he lay.

'Fair Proserpina,' quoth she,
'Shall not have thee yet from me;
Nor thy soul to fly begin,
While my lips can keep it in.'

Here she ceased again. And some
Say Apollo would have come
To have cured his wounded limb,
But that she had smothered him.

WILLIAM BROWNE OF TAVISTOCK

Adonis was wounded by a wild boar.
  From his blood sprang the rose, from
  Venus' tears the wind-flower (anem-
  one)
Proserpina: queen of the nether world
Apollo: here, in his attribute of physi-
  cian

SANTORIN

(*A Legend of the Aegean*)

'Who are you, Sea Lady,
And where in the seas are we?
I have too long been steering
By the flashes in your eyes.
Why drops the moonlight through my heart,
And why so quietly
Go the great engines of my boat
As if their souls were free?'
'Oh ask me not, bold sailor;
Is not your ship a magic ship
That sails without a sail:

Are not these isles the Isles of Greece
And dust upon the sea?
But answer me three questions
And give me answers three.
What is your ship?' 'A British.'
'And where may Britain be?'
'Oh it lies north, dear lady;
It is a small country.'
'Yet you will know my lover,
Though you live far away:
And you will whisper where he has gone,
That lily boy to look upon
And whiter than the spray.'
'How should I know your lover,
Lady of the sea?'
'Alexander, Alexander,
The King of the World was he.'
'Weep not for him, dear lady,
But come aboard my ship.
So many years ago he died,
He's dead as dead can be.'
'O base and brutal sailor
To lie this lie to me.
His mother was the foam-foot
Star-sparkling Aphrodite;
His father was Adonis
Who lives away in Lebanon,
In stony Lebanon, where blooms
His red anemone.
But where is Alexander,
The soldier Alexander,
My golden love of olden days
The King of the world and me?'

She sank into the moonlight
And the sea was only sea.

JAMES ELROY FLECKER

CLEOPATRA

ENOBARBUS

The barge she sat in, like a burnish'd throne,
Burn'd on the water; the poop was beaten gold,
Purple the sails, and so perfumed, that
The winds were love-sick with them, the oars were silver,
Which to the tune of flutes kept stroke, and made
The water which they beat to follow faster,
As amorous of their strokes. For her own person,
It beggar'd all description; she did lie
In her pavilion,—cloth-of-gold of tissue,—
O'er-picturing that Venus where we see
The fancy outwork nature; on each side her
Stood pretty-dimpled boys, like smiling Cupids,
With divers-colour'd fans, whose wind did seem
To glow the delicate cheeks which they did cool,
And what they undid did.

AGRIPPA

O! rare for Antony.

ENOBARBUS

Her gentlewomen, like the Nereides,
So many mermaids, tended her i' the eyes,
And made their bends adornings; at the helm
A seeming mermaid steers; the silken tackle
Swell with the touches of those flower-soft hands,
That yarely frame the office. From the barge
A strange invisible perfume hits the sense
Of the adjacent wharfs. The city cast
Her people out upon her, and Antony,
Enthron'd i' the market-place, did sit alone,
Whistling to the air; which, but for vacancy,
Had gone to gaze on Cleopatra too
And made a gap in nature.

AGRIPPA

Rare Egyptian!

ENOBARBUS

Upon her landing, Antony sent to her,
Invited her to supper; she replied
It should be better he became her guest,
Which she entreated. Our courteous Antony,
Whom ne'er the word of 'No' woman heard speak,
Being barber'd ten times o'er, goes to the feast,
And, for his ordinary pays his heart
For what his eyes eat only.

AGRIPPA

Royal wench!
She made great Caesar lay his sword to bed;
He plough'd her, and she cropp'd.

ENOBARBUS

I saw her once
Hop forty paces through the public street;
And having lost her breath, she spoke, and panted
That she did make defect perfection,
And, breathless, power breathe forth.

MECAENAS

Now Antony must leave her utterly.

ENOBARBUS

Never; he will not:
Age cannot wither her, nor custom stale
Her infinite variety; other women cloy
The appetites they feed, but she makes hungry
Where most she satisfies.

WILLIAM SHAKESPEARE

LAKES

Last, last of all, in this high night of dews,
late searching through old, fabulous Mays,
I picture you, Isolde! deluded, as you touch
under the sheet a cold, an icy sword . . .

Loyal . . . disloyal? O sorry, sorry blade!
offence to love, insidious, and how much more
if, tenderly, an echo of the Latin Muse
whisper *O sweet sweet is the sleep of lovers* . . .

O Latin wisdom! What a pupil,
what a poor pupil your life-giving bosom
nourished in me, who still half-dreaming waits
for her to return once more to longing autumn . . .

In vain the beech spreads its clear shining gold . . .
in vain the maple reddens every bough . . .
no more will you loosen your golden hair
over the clear, the cold crystal lakes . . .

How ever forget the name of her
who so loved autumn? Ever in their plaint
the leaves repeat it over, and the wind:
Where are you? O where are you? where . . .

And now I waken, as the cock cries harsh . . .
I feel, and grope . . . 'Where are you, sweet one?'
I am here . . . I am here . . . The cold wave has taken me . . .
I am here . . . fainting . . . in the crystal lakes . . .

All is now still . . . but suddenly a horse
far in the valley neighs . . . or does it laugh?
I am here . . . I am here . . . Don't let me die . . .
I am here weeping by the crystal lakes . . .

And now dawn sparkles in the coral skies . . .
I call and call . . . and no voice answers me . . .

I am here I am here I am the last the Fair One
I am cold at the bottom of the crystal lakes . . .

FRANCESCO BIANCO

FIDELE

To fair Fidele's grassy tomb
  Soft maids and village hinds shall bring
Each opening sweet of earliest bloom,
  And rifle all the breathing Spring.

No wailing ghost shall dare appear
  To vex with shrieks this quiet grove;
But shepherd lads assemble here,
  And melting virgins own their love.

No wither'd witch shall here be seen,
  No goblins lead their nightly crew;
The female fays shall haunt the green,
  And dress thy grave with pearly dew.

The redbreast oft at evening hours
  Shall kindly lend his little aid,
With hoary moss, and gather'd flowers,
  To deck the ground where thou art laid.

When howling winds, and beating rain,
  In tempests shake thy sylvan cell;
Or 'midst the chase, on every plain,
  The tender thought on thee shall dwell;

Each lonely scene shall thee restore,
  For thee the tear be duly shed;
Beloved, till life can charm no more;
  And mourn'd, till Pity's self be dead.

WILLIAM COLLINS

SONNET XLI: THE TOURNAMENT, 1581

Having this day my horse, my hand, my lance
Guided so well that I obtained the prize,
Both by the judgment of the English eyes,
And of some sent from that sweet enemy, France,
Horsemen my skill in horsemanship advance,
Town-folks my strength; a daintier judge applies
His praise to sleight which from good use doth rise;
Some lucky wits impute it but to chance;
Others, because of both sides I do take
My blood from them who did excel in this,
Think nature me a man-at-arms did make.
How far they shoot awry! The true cause is,
Stella looked on, and from her heavenly face
Sent forth the beams which made so fair my race.

SIR PHILIP SIDNEY

THE HENCHMAN

My lady walks her morning round,
My lady's page her fleet greyhound,
My lady's hair the fond winds stir,
And all the birds make songs for her.

Her thrushes sing in Rathburn bowers,
And Rathburn side is gay with flowers;
But ne'er like hers, in flower or bird,
Was beauty seen or music heard.

Oh, proud and calm!—she cannot know
Where'er she goes with her I go;
Oh, cold and fair—she cannot guess
I kneel to share her hound's caress!

The hound and I are on her trail,
The wind and I uplift her veil;
As if the calm, cold moon she were,
And I the tide, I follow her.

As unrebuked as they, I share
The license of the sun and air,
And in a common homage hide
My worship from her scorn and pride.

No lance have I, in joust or fight,
To splinter in my lady's sight;
But, at her feet, how blest were I
For any need of hers to die!

JOHN GREENLEAF WHITTIER

Henchman: page of honor, squire

LA BELLE DAME SANS MERCI

O what can ail thee, knight-at-arms,
    Alone and palely loitering?
The sedge has wither'd from the lake,
    And no birds sing.

O what can ail thee, knight-at-arms,
    So haggard and so woe-begone?
The squirrel's granary is full,
    And the harvest's done.

I see a lily on thy brow
    With anguish moist and fever dew
And on thy cheeks a fading rose
    Fast withereth too.

I met a lady in the meads,
    Full beautiful—a faery's child,
Her hair was long, her foot was light,
    And her eyes were wild.

I made a garland for her head,
  And bracelets too, and fragrant zone;
She look'd at me as she did love,
  And made sweet moan.

I set her on my pacing steed,
  And nothing else saw all day long,
For sidelong would she bend, and sing
  A faery's song.

She found me roots of relish sweet,
  And honey wild, and manna dew,
And sure in language strange she said,
  'I love thee true.'

She took me to her elfin grot,
  And there she wept, and sigh'd full sore,
And there I shut her wild wild eyes
  With kisses four.

And there she lullèd me asleep
  And there I dream'd—Ah! woe betide!
The latest dream I ever dream'd
  On the cold hill side.

I saw pale kings, and princes too,
  Pale warriors, death-pale were they all;
They cried—'La belle Dame sans Merci
  Hath thee in thrall!'

I saw their starved lips in the gloam
  With horrid warning gapèd wide,
And I awoke and found me here
  On the cold hill's side.

And this is why I sojourn here
  Alone and palely loitering,
Though the sedge is wither'd from the lake,
  And no birds sing.

JOHN KEATS

A GARDEN BY THE SEA

I know a little garden-close
Set thick with lily and red rose,
Where I would wander if I might
From dewy dawn to dewy night,
And have one with me wandering.

And though within it no birds sing,
And though no pillar'd house is there,
And though the apple boughs are bare
Of fruit and blossom, would to God,
Her feet upon the green grass trod,
And I beheld them as before!

There comes a murmur from the shore,
And in the place two fair streams are,
Drawn from the purple hills afar,
Drawn down unto the restless sea;
The hills whose flowers ne'er fed the bee,
The shore no ship has ever seen,
Still beaten by the billows green,
Whose murmur comes unceasingly
Unto the place for which I cry.

For which I cry both day and night,
For which I let slip all delight,
That maketh me both deaf and blind,
Careless to win, unskill'd to find,
And quick to lose what all men seek.

Yet tottering as I am, and weak,
Still have I left a little breath
To seek within the jaws of death
An entrance to that happy place;
To seek the unforgotten face
Once seen, once kiss'd, once reft from me
Anigh the murmuring of the sea.

WILLIAM MORRIS

THE SONG OF WANDERING AENGUS

I went out to the hazel wood,
Because a fire was in my head,
And cut and peeled a hazel wand,
And hooked a berry to a thread;
And when white moths were on the wing,
And moth-like stars were flickering out,
I dropped the berry in a stream
And caught a little silver trout.

When I had laid it on the floor
I went to blow the fire aflame,
But something rustled on the floor,
And some one called me by my name:
It had become a glimmering girl
With apple blossom in her hair
Who called me by my name and ran
And faded through the brightening air.

Though I am old with wandering
Through hollow lands and hilly lands,
I will find out where she has gone,
And kiss her lips and take her hands;
And walk among long dappled grass,
And pluck till time and times are done
The silver apples of the moon,
The golden apples of the sun.

WILLIAM BUTLER YEATS

ANNABEL LEE

It was many and many a year ago,
  In a kingdom by the sea,
That a maiden there lived whom you may know
  By the name of ANNABEL LEE;
And this maiden she lived with no other thought
  Than to love and be loved by me.

I was a child and *she* was a child,
   In this kingdom by the sea:
But we loved with a love that was more than love—
   I and my ANNABEL LEE;
With a love that the winged seraphs of heaven
   Coveted her and me.

And this was the reason that, long ago,
   In this kingdom by the sea,
A wind blew out of a cloud, chilling
   My beautiful ANNABEL LEE;
So that her high-born kinsman came
   And bore her away from me,
To shut her up in a sepulchre
   In this kingdom by the sea.

The angels, not half so happy in heaven,
   Went envying her and me—
Yes!—that was the reason (as all men know,
   In this kingdom by the sea)
That the wind came out of the cloud by night,
   Chilling and killing my ANNABEL LEE.

But our love it was stronger by far than the love
   Of those who were older than we—
   Of many far wiser than we—
And neither the angels in heaven above,
   Nor the demons down under the sea,
Can ever dissever my soul from the soul
   Of the beautiful ANNABEL LEE.

For the moon never beams, without bringing me dreams
   Of the beautiful ANNABEL LEE;
And the stars never rise, but I feel the bright eyes
   Of the beautiful ANNABEL LEE;
And so, all the night-tide, I lie down by the side
Of my darling—my darling—my life and my bride,

In the sepulchre there by the sea,
In her tomb by the sounding sea.

EDGAR ALLAN POE

ALL IN GREEN WENT MY LOVE RIDING

All in green went my love riding
on a great horse of gold
into the silver dawn.

four lean hounds crouched low and smiling
the merry deer ran before.

Fleeter be they than dappled dreams
the swift sweet deer
the red rare deer.

Four red roebuck at a white water
the cruel bugle sang before.

Horn at hip went my love riding
riding the echo down
into the silver dawn.

four lean hounds crouched low and smiling
the level meadows ran before.

Softer be they than slippered sleep
the lean lithe deer
the fleet flown deer.

Four fleet does at a gold valley
the famished arrow sang before.

Bow at belt went my love riding
riding the mountain down
into the silver dawn.

four lean hounds crouched low and smiling
the sheer peaks ran before.

Paler be they than daunting death
the sleek slim deer
the tall tense deer.

Four tall stags at a green mountain
the lucky hunter sang before.

All in green went my love riding
on a great horse of gold
into the silver dawn.

four lean hounds crouched low and smiling
my heart fell dead before.

E. E. CUMMINGS

❧ ❦

ALAS

One moment take thy rest.
Out of mere nought in space
Beauty moved human breast
To tell in this far face
A dream in noonday seen,
Never to fade or pass:
A breath-time's mute delight:
   A joy in flight:
The aught desire doth mean,
    Sighing, Alas!

WALTER DE LA MARE

this far face: a drawing by Pamela
Bianco

✑ NOTES ✑

Cummings's "All in green went my love riding" first appeared in
The Harvard Monthly. (For an account of another student poet's appearance in that publication, see notes to Section 11.) Cummings also
wrote "Tumbling-hair" at Harvard, unaware until many years later of
its resemblance to Milton's Proserpine (here, in "Adam and Eve,"
starting at the fifth line, all the passages being taken from Book IV
of *Paradise Lost*). The word Nicean" in Poe's poem "To Helen" appears to be a variation of Milton's "Nyseian" in the passage referred
to, from the nymphs who brought up Bacchus and were rewarded by
Jupiter by being placed among the stars—themselves the Hyades. As
for Poe's final stanza, Hervey Allen believed that the poet, calling one
evening, saw Mrs. Helen Stannard as described, with the lighted lamp
in her hand. American troops took Enna, in Sicily, in World War II.

Like Edward Thomas (p. 253), Francis Ledwidge died in World
War I, aged twenty-six. He was born at Slane, County Meath, Ireland,
and, though a strong nationalist, joined up with the Royal Inniskillings
in 1914, "neither for a principle, nor a people, nor a law, but for the
fields along the Boyne, for the birds and the blue sky over them." His
Complete Poems appeared in 1919.

The source of Shakespeare's Cleopatra is Plutarch, who was translated into French by Bishop Jacques Amyot and thence into English by
Sir Thomas North, who appears to have consulted the Greek text as
well. But "without Amyot, Sir Thomas North could not have written—
North, whose words stirred Shakespeare's imagination more deeply than
it was stirred by those of any other man, save possibly Marlowe"
(F. O. Matthiessen, *Translation: An Elizabethan Art,* Harvard University Press, 1931; p. 57). North's *Plutarch's Lives* appeared in 1579,
and is the source of the Roman plays of Shakespeare. The description of
Cleopatra on her barge occurs in the life of Marcus Antonius:

> . . . Caesar and Pompey knew her when she was but a young thing,
> and knew not then what the world meant: but now she went to An-
> tonius at the age when a woman's beauty is at the prime, and she also of
> best judgment.
> So she furnished herself with a world of gifts, store of gold and sil-
> ver, and of riches and other sumptuous ornaments as is credible enough

she might bring from so great a house, and from so wealthy and rich a realm as Egypt was. But yet she carried nothing with her wherein she trusted more than in herself, and in the charms and enchantment of her passing beauty and grace.

Therefore, when she was sent unto by divers letters, both from Antonius himself, and also from his friends, she made so light of it, and mocked Antonius so much, that she disdained to set forward otherwise, but to take her barge in the river of Cydnus, the poop whereof was of gold, the sails of purple, and the oars of silver, which kept stroke in rowing after the sound of the music of flutes, hautboys, zitherns, viols, and such other instruments as they played upon in the barge.

And now for the person of herself: she was laid under a pavilion of cloth of gold of tissue, apparelled and attired like the goddess Venus, commonly drawn in picture: and hard by her, on either hand of her, pretty, fair boys apparelled as painters do set forth god Cupid, with little fans in their hands, with the which they fanned wind upon her. Her ladies and gentlewomen also, the fairest of them, were apparelled like the Nymphs—Nereides, which are the mermaids of the waters—and like the Graces; some steering the helm, others tending the tackle and ropes of the barge, out of the which there came a wonderful passing sweet savor of perfumes, that perfumed the wharf's side. . . .

The literary source of William Collins' "Fidele" is the more famous poem, or song, in *Cymbeline*, Act IV, Scene 2. The situation is complex —Imogen, daughter of the King of Roman Britain, but known as Fidele, is brought in, supposedly dead, by Arviragus, disguised as Polydore, to his brother Guiderius, now called Cadwal, her half-brothers:

GUIDERIUS

O, sweetest, fairest lily!
My brother wears thee not the one half so well
As when thou grew'st thyself. . . .

ARVIRAGUS

With fairest flowers
While summer lasts and I live here, Fidele,
I'll sweeten thy sad grave. . . .

Then Guiderius and Arviragus sing together:

Fear no more the heat o' the sun,
Nor the furious winter's rages;
Thou thy worldly task hast done,
Home art gone, and ta'en thy wages;

> Golden lads and girls all must,
> As chimney-sweepers, come to dust.

A sword in the bed was a medieval symbol of chastity ("Lakes").
Bianco's "echo of the Latin Muse" in the same poem is a reference to
this passage in Ovid:

> Now in her tender arms I sweetly bide;
> If ever, now well lies she by my side;
> The air is cold, and sleep is sweetest now,
> And birds send forth shrill notes from every bough

(Elegy 13, translated by Marlowe).

"A Garden by the Sea" is an extract from a much longer work by
Morris, *The Life and Death of Jason.* As for "The Song of Wandering
Aengus," which resembles it, it seems a subject made to a choreog-
rapher's hand.

There is also a curious resemblance in Poe's "Annabel Lee" to a
poem by John Sheffield, Duke of Buckinghamshire. The poem is called
"On One Who Died Discovering Her Kindness," the word "discovering" here meaning "revealing":

> Some vex their souls with jealous pain,
> While others sigh for cold disdain:
> Love's various slaves we daily see—
> Yet happy all compared with me!
>
> Of all mankind I loved the best
> A nymph so far above the rest
> That we outshined the blest above,
> In beauty she, as I in love.
>
> And therefore they, who could not bear
> To be outdone by mortals here,
> Among themselves have placed her now,
> And left me wretched here below.
>
> All other fate I could have borne,
> And e'en endured her very scorn;
> But oh! thus all at once to find
> That dread account—both dead and kind!
> What heart can hold? If yet I live,
> 'Tis but to show how much I grieve.

4.

Homage to Shakespeare

4. HOMAGE TO SHAKESPEARE

ON MR. WM. SHAKESPEARE

Renownèd Spenser, lie a thought more nigh
To learnèd Chaucer; and rare Beaumont, lie
A little nearer Spenser, to make room
For Shakespeare in your three-fold four-fold tomb.
To lodge all four in one bed make a shift
Until Doomsday; for hardly will a fift[h],
Betwixt this day and that, by fate be slain,
For whom your curtains may be drawn again.

If your precedency in death doth bar
A fourth place in your sacred sepulcher,
Under this carvèd marble of thine own,
Sleep, rare tragedian, Shakespeare, sleep alone:
Thy unmolested peace, unsharèd cave,
Possess as lord, not tenant, of thy grave,
That unto us and others it may be
Honor hereafter to be laid by thee.

WILLIAM BASSE

Shakespeare was buried, April 25, 1616, in Holy Trin-
ity Church, Stratford, where he had been baptized
April 26, 1564. The tombs of Chaucer, Spenser and
Beaumont are in Westminster Abbey

TO THE MEMORY OF MY BELOVED, THE
AUTHOR MR. WILLIAM SHAKESPEARE:
And What He Hath Left Us

To draw no envy, Shakespeare, on thy name,
    Am I thus ample to thy book and fame,
While I confess thy writings to be such
    As neither man nor Muse can praise too much;
'Tis true, and all men's suffrage. But these ways
    Were not the paths I meant unto thy praise,
For silliest ignorance on these may light,
    Which, when it sounds at best, but echoes right;
Or blind affection, which doth ne'er advance
    The truth, but gropes, and urgeth all by chance;
Or crafty malice might pretend this praise,
    And think to ruin where it seemed to raise.
These are, as some infamous bawd or whore
    Should praise a matron—what could hurt her more?
But thou art proof against them, and indeed
    Above th' ill fortune of them or the need.
I therefore will begin. Soul of the Age!
    The applause! delight! the wonder of our stage!
My Shakespeare, rise. I will not lodge thee by
    Chaucer, or Spenser, or bid Beaumont lie
A little further, to make thee a room:
    Thou art a monument without a tomb,
And art alive still while thy book doth live,
    And we have wits to read and praise to give.
That I not mix thee so, my brain excuses,
    I mean with great but disproportioned Muses;
For if I thought my judgment were of years,
    I should commit thee surely with thy peers,
And tell how far thou didst our Lyly outshine,
    Or sporting Kyd, or Marlowe's mighty line;
And though thou hadst small Latin and less Greek,

From thence to honor thee I would not seek
For names, but call forth thund'ring Aeschylus,
   Euripides and Sophocles to us,
Pacuvius, Accius, him of Cordova dead,
   To life again to hear thy buskin tread,
And shake a stage; or, when thy socks were on,
   Leave thee alone for the comparison
Of all that insolent Greece or haughty Rome
   Sent forth or since did from their ashes come.
Triumph, my Britain, thou hast one to show
   To whom all scenes of Europe homage owe;
He was not of an age, but for all time!
   And all the Muses still were in their prime
When like Apollo he came forth to warm
   Our ears, or like a Mercury to charm!
Nature herself was proud of his designs,
   And joyed to wear the dressing of his lines!
Which were so richly spun, and woven so fit,
   As, since, she will vouchsafe no other wit.
The merry Greek, tart Aristophanes,
   Neat Terence, witty Plautus, now not please,
But antiquated and deserted lie
   As they were not of Nature's family.
Yet must I not give Nature all: thy art,
   My gentle Shakespeare, must enjoy a part,
For though the poet's matter Nature be,
   His art doth give the fashion, and that he
Who casts to write a living line must sweat
   (Such as thine are) and strike the second heat
Upon the Muses' anvil, turn the same
   (And himself with it) that he thinks to frame,
Or for the laurel he may gain a scorn,
   For a good poet's made as well as born;
And such wert thou. Look how the father's face
   Lives in his issue; even so, the race
Of Shakespeare's mind and manners brightly shines
   In his well-turnèd and true-filèd lines,

In each of which he seems to shake a lance,
  As brandished at the eyes of ignorance.
Sweet Swan of Avon! what a sight it were
  To see thee in our waters yet appear,
And make those flights upon the banks of Thames
  That so did take Eliza and our James!
But stay, I see thee in the hemisphere
  Advanced and made a constellation there!
Shine forth, thou star of poets, and with rage,
  Or influence, chide or cheer the drooping stage,
Which since thy flight from hence hath mourned like night,
  And despairs day, but for thy volume's light.

BEN JONSON

him of Cordova dead: Seneca
buskin: tragedy
socks: comedies
scenes: stages

TO THE MEMORY
OF THE DECEASED AUTHOR
MASTER W. SHAKESPEARE

Shakespeare, at length thy pious fellows give
The world thy works: thy works by which outlive
Thy tomb thy name must, when that stone is rent
And Time dissolves thy Stratford monument.
Here, we alive shall view thee still; this book,
When brass and marble fade, shall make thee look
Fresh to all ages; when posterity
Shall loathe what's new, think all is prodigy
That is not Shakespeare's, ev'ry line, each verse,
Here shall revive, redeem thee from thy hearse.
Nor fire, nor cankering age, as Naso said
Of his, thy wit-fraught book shall once invade,

Nor shall I e'er believe or think thee dead
(Though missed) until our bankrupt stage be sped
(Impossible) with some new strain t' out-do
Passions of Juliet and her Romeo,
Or till I hear a scene more nobly take
Than when thy half-sword parleying Romans spake.
Till these, till any of thy volume's rest
Shall with more fire, more feeling be exprest,
Be sure, our Shakespeare, thou canst never die,
But, crowned with laurel, live eternally.

LEONARD DIGGES

fellows: fellow actors
Stratford monument: Shakespeare's bust in Holy Trinity
    Church
this book: the First Folio, 1623
Naso: Ovid
half-sword: short sword developed by Romans for close
    combat

❧ ❦

TO THE MEMORY OF M[ASTER]
W. SHAKESPEARE

We wondered, Shakespeare, that thou went'st so soon
From the world's stage to the grave's tiring-room.
We thought thee dead; but this, thy printed worth,
Tells thy spectators that thou went'st but forth
To enter with applause. An actor's art
Can die, and live to act a second part;
That's but an exit of mortality,
This a re-entrance to a plaudity.

I. M.

tiring-room: dressing room, from attiring

UPON THE LINES AND LIFE
OF THE FAMOUS SCENIC POET,
MASTER WILLIAM SHAKESPEARE

Those hands, which you so clapped, go now and wring,
You Britons brave, for done are Shakespeare's days;
His days are done that made the dainty plays
Which made the globe of heav'n and earth to ring;
Dried is that vein, dried is the Thespian spring,
Turned all to tears, and Phoebus clouds his rays;
That corpse, that coffin, now bestick those bays
Which crowned him poet first, then poets' king.
If tragedies might any prologue have,
All those he made would scarce make one to this,
Where Fame, now that he gone is to the grave
(Death's public tiring-house) the nuncius is.
    For though his line of life went soon about,
    The life yet of his lines shall never out.

HUGH HOLLAND

globe: a pun on the Globe Theatre, where Shakespeare's plays
  were performed
bays: wreath made of bay leaves
nuncius: messenger

᠉ ᠊

AN EPITAPH ON THE ADMIRABLE
DRAMATIC POET, WILLIAM SHAKESPEARE

What needs my Shakespeare for his honored bones
The labor of an age in pilèd stones?
Or that his hallowed relics should be hid
Under a star-ypointing pyramid?
Dear son of memory, great heir of fame,

What need'st thou such weak witness of thy name?
Thou, in our wonder and astonishment,
Hast built thyself a livelong monument;
For whilst, to the shame of slow-endeavoring art,
Thy easy numbers flow, and that each heart
Hath, from the leaves of thy unvalued book,
Those Delphic lines with deep impression took,
Then thou, our fancy of itself bereaving,
Dost make us marble with too much conceiving,
And, so sepulchered, in such pomp dost lie,
That kings for such a tomb would wish to die.

JOHN MILTON

star-ypointing: pointing to the stars
Delphic: oracular

SHAKESPEARE

Others abide our question. Thou art free,
We ask and ask: Thou smilest and art still,
Out-topping knowledge. For the loftiest hill
That to the stars uncrowns his majesty,
Planting his steadfast footsteps in the sea,
Making the heaven of heavens his dwelling-place,
Spares but the cloudy border of his base
To the foil'd searching of mortality;
And thou, who didst the stars and sunbeams know,
Self-school'd, self-scann'd, self-honor'd, self-secure,
Didst walk on earth unguess'd at. Better so!
All pains the immortal spirit must endure,
   All weakness that impairs, all griefs that bow,
   Find their sole voice in that victorious brow.

MATTHEW ARNOLD

THE SONNETS: A SELECTION

Being your slave, what should I do but tend
Upon the hours and times of your desire?
I have no precious time at all to spend,
Nor services to do, till you require.
Nor dare I chide the world-without-end hour
Whilst I, my sovereign, watch the clock for you,
Nor think the bitterness of absence sour
When you have bid your servant once adieu;
Nor dare I question with my jealous thought
Where you may be, or your affairs suppose,
But, like a sad slave, stay and think of nought,
Save, where you are how happy you make those.
  So true a fool is love that in your will,
  Though you do anything, he thinks no ill.

When I have seen by Time's fell hand defac'd
The rich-proud cost of outworn buried age;
When sometimes lofty towers I see down-raz'd,
And brass eternal slave to mortal rage;
When I have seen the hungry ocean gain
Advantage on the kingdom of the shore,
And the firm soil win of the watery main,
Increasing store with loss, and loss with store;
When I have seen such interchange of state,
Or state itself confounded to decay;
Ruin hath taught me thus to ruminate—
That Time will come and take my love away.
  This thought is as a death, which cannot choose
  But weep to have that which it fears to lose.

Since brass, nor stone, nor earth, nor boundless sea,
But sad mortality o'ersways their power,
How with this rage shall beauty hold a plea,

Whose action is no stronger than a flower?
O! how shall summer's honey breath hold out
Against the wrackful siege of battering days,
When rocks impregnable are not so stout,
Nor gates of steel so strong, but Time decays?
O fearful meditation! where, alack,
Shall Time's best jewel from Time's chest lie hid?
Or what strong hand can hold his swift foot back?
Or who his spoil of beauty can forbid?
   O! none, unless this miracle have might,
   That in black ink my love may still shine bright.

Tir'd with all these, for restful death I cry
As to behold the heart a beggar born,
And needy nothing trimm'd in jollity,
And purest faith unhappily forsworn,
And gilded honour shamefully misplac'd,
And maiden virtue rudely strumpeted,
And right perfection wrongfully disgraced,
And strength by limping sway disabled,
And art made tongue-tied by authority,
And folly—doctor-like—controlling skill,
And simple truth miscall'd simplicity,
And captive good attending captain ill:
   Tir'd with all these, from these I would be gone,
   Save that, to die, I leave my love alone.

That time of year thou mayst in me behold
When yellow leaves, or none, or few, do hang
Upon those boughs which shake against the cold,
Bare ruin'd choirs, where late the sweet birds sang.
In me thou see'st the twilight of such day
As after sunset fadeth in the west;
Which by and by black night doth take away,
Death's second self, that seals up all in rest.
In me thou see'st the glowing of such fire,
That on the ashes of his youth doth lie,

As the death-bed whereon it must expire
Consum'd with that which it was nourish'd by.
   This thou perceiv'st, which makes thy love more strong,
   To love that well which thou must leave ere long.

Why is my verse so barren of new pride,
So far from variation or quick change?
Why with the time do I not glance aside
To new-found methods and to compounds strange?
Why write I still all one, ever the same,
And keep invention in a noted weed,
That every word doth almost tell my name,
Showing their birth, and where they did proceed?
O! know, sweet love, I always write of you,
And you and love are still my argument;
So all my best is dressing old words new,
Spending again what is already spent:
   For as the sun is daily new and old,
   So is my love still telling what is told.

Farewell! thou art too dear for my possessing,
And like enough thou know'st thy estimate:
The charter of thy worth gives thee releasing;
My bonds in thee are all determinate.
For how do I hold thee but by thy granting?
And for that riches where is my deserving?
The cause of this fair gift in me is wanting,
And so my patent back again is swerving.
Thyself thou gav'st, thy own worth then not knowing,
Or me, to whom thou gav'st it, else mistaking;
So thy great gift, upon misprision growing,
Comes home again, on better judgment making.
   Thus have I had thee, as a dream doth flatter,
   In sleep a king, but, waking, no such matter.

When thou shalt be dispos'd to set me light,
And place my merit in the eye of scorn,

Upon thy side against myself I'll fight,
And prove thee virtuous, though thou art forsworn.
With mine own weakness, being best acquainted,
Upon thy part I can set down a story
Of faults conceal'd, wherein I am attainted,
That thou in losing me shalt win much glory:
And I by this will be a gainer too;
For bending all my loving thoughts on thee,
The injuries that to myself I do,
Doing thee vantage, double-vantage me.
    Such is my love, to thee I so belong,
      That for thy right myself will bear all wrong.

Say that thou didst forsake me for some fault,
And I will comment upon that offence:
Speak of my lameness, and I straight will halt,
Against thy reasons making no defence.
Thou canst not, love, disgrace me half so ill,
To set a form upon desired change,
As I'll myself disgrace; knowing thy will,
I will acquaintance strangle, and look strange;
Be absent from thy walks; and in my tongue
Thy sweet beloved name no more thall dwell,
Lest I, too much profane, should do it wrong,
And haply of our old acquaintance tell.
    For thee, against myself I'll vow debate,
      For I must ne'er love him whom thou dost hate.

Then hate me when thou wilt; if ever, now;
Now, while the world is bent my deeds to cross,
Join with the spite of fortune, make me bow,
And do not drop in for an after-loss:
Ah! do not, when my heart hath 'scaped this sorrow,
Come in the rearward of a conquer'd woe;
Give not a windy night a rainy morrow,
To linger out a purpos'd overthrow.
If thou wilt leave me, do not leave me last,

When other petty griefs have done their spite,
But in the onset come: so shall I taste
At first the very worst of fortune's might;
    And other strains of woe, which now seem woe,
    Compar'd with loss of thee will not seem so.

How like a winter hath my absence been
From thee, the pleasure of the fleeting year!
What freezings have I felt, what dark days seen!
What old December's bareness everywhere!
And yet this time remov'd was summer's time;
The teeming autumn, big with rich increase,
Bearing the wanton burden of the prime,
Like widow'd wombs after their lords' decease:
Yet this abundant issue seem'd to me
But hope of orphans and unfather'd fruit;
For summer and his pleasures wait on thee,
And, thou away, the very birds are mute:
    Or, if they sing, 'tis with so dull a cheer,
    That leaves look pale, dreading the winter's near.

My love is strengthen'd, though more weak in seeming;
I love not less, though less the show appear:
That love is merchantiz'd whose rich esteeming
The owner's tongue doth publish everywhere.
Our love was new, and then but in the spring,
When I was wont to greet it with my lays;
As Philomel in summer's front doth sing,
And stops her pipe in growth of riper days:
Not that the summer is less pleasant now
Than when her mournful hymns did hush the night,
But that wild music burthens every bough,
And sweets grown common lose their dear delight.
    Therefore, like her, I sometime hold my tongue,
    Because I would not dull you with my song.

Alack! what poverty my Muse brings forth,
That having such a scope to show her pride,
The argument, all bare, is of more worth
Than when it hath my added praise beside!
O! blame me not, if I no more can write!
Look in your glass, and there appears a face
That over-goes my blunt invention quite,
Dulling my lines and doing me disgrace.
Were it not sinful then, striving to mend,
To mar the subject that before was well?
For to no other pass my verses tend
Than of your graces and your gifts to tell;
　　And more, much more, than in my verse can sit,
　　Your own glass shows you when you look in it.

When in the chronicle of wasted time
I see descriptions of the fairest wights,
And beauty making beautiful old rime,
In praise of ladies dead and lovely knights,
Then, in the blazon of sweet beauty's best,
Of hand, of foot, of lip, of eye, or brow,
I see their antique pen would have express'd
Even such a beauty as you master now.
So all their praises are but prophecies
Of this our time, all you prefiguring;
And, for they look'd but with divining eyes,
They had not skill enough your worth to sing:
　　For we, which now behold these present days,
　　Have eyes to wonder, but lack tongues to praise.

O! never say that I was false of heart,
Though absence seem'd my flame to qualify.
As easy might I from myself depart
As from my soul, which in thy breast doth lie.
That is my home of love: if I have rang'd,
Like him that travels, I return again;
Just to the time, not with the time exchang'd,

So that myself bring water for my stain.
Never believe, though in my nature reign'd
All frailties that besiege all kinds of blood,
That it could so preposterously be stain'd
To leave for nothing all thy sum of good;
   For nothing this wide universe I call,
   Save thou, my rose; in it thou art my all.

Let me not to the marriage of true minds
Admit impediments. Love is not love
Which alters when it alteration finds,
Or bends with the remover to remove:
O, no! it is an ever-fixed mark,
That looks on tempests and is never shaken;
It is the star to every wandering bark,
Whose worth's unknown, although his height be taken.
Love's not Time's fool, though rosy lips and cheeks
Within his bending sickle's compass come;
Love alters not with his brief hours and weeks,
But bears it out even to the edge of doom.
   If this be error, and upon me prov'd,
   I never writ, nor no man ever lov'd.

WILLIAM SHAKESPEARE

SCORN NOT THE SONNET

Scorn not the Sonnet; Critic, you have frowned,
Mindless of its just honors; with this key
Shakespeare unlocked his heart; the melody
Of this small lute gave ease to Petrarch's wound;
A thousand times this pipe did Tasso sound;
With it Camöens soothed an exile's grief;

The Sonnet glittered a gay myrtle leaf
Amid the cypress with which Dante crowned
His visionary brow: a glow-worm lamp,
It cheered mild Spenser, called from Faery-land
To struggle through dark ways; and, when a damp
Fell round the path of Milton, in his hand
The Thing became a trumpet; whence he blew
Soul-animating strains—alas, too few!

WILLIAM WORDSWORTH

≥ ≤

HOUSE: A REPLY

Shall I sonnet-sing to you about myself?
    Do I live in a house you would like to see?
Is it scant of gear, has it store of pelf?
    'Unlock my heart with a sonnet-key?'

Invite the world, as my betters have done?
    'Take notice: this building remains on view,
Its suites of reception every one,
    Its private apartment and bedroom too;

'For a ticket, apply to the publisher.'
    No: thanking the public, I must decline.
A peep through my window, if folk prefer;
    But, please you, no foot over threshold of mine!

I have mixed with a crowd and heard free talk
    In a foreign land where an earthquake chanced:
And a house stood gaping, nought to balk
    Man's eye wherever he gazed or glanced.

The whole of the frontage shaven sheer,
    The inside gaped: exposed to day,

Right and wrong and common and queer,
    Bare, as the palm of your hand, it lay.

The owner? Oh, he had been crushed, no doubt!
    'Odd tables and chairs for a man of wealth!
What a parcel of musty old books about!
    He smoked,—no wonder he lost his health!

'I doubt if he bathed before he dressed.
    A brasier?—the pagan, he burned perfumes!
You see it is proved, what the neighbors guessed:
    His wife and himself had separate rooms.'

Friends, the goodman of the house at least
    Kept house to himself till an earthquake came:
'Tis the fall of its frontage permits you feast
    On the inside arrangement you praise or blame.

Outside should suffice for evidence:
    And whoso desires to penetrate
Deeper, must dive by the spirit-sense—
    No optics like yours, at any rate!

'Hoity toity! A street to explore,
    Your house the exception! *"With this same key
Shakespeare unlocked his heart,"* once more!'
    Did Shakespeare? If so, the less Shakespeare he!

ROBERT BROWNING

❧ NOTES ❧

Facing the Martin Droeshout engraving of a portrait of Shakespeare on the title page of the First Folio, 1623, is a conventional portrait verse by Ben Jonson ("conventional," because there are similar ones in other poets' works):

> This figure, that thou here seest put,
>   It was for gentle Shakespeare cut;
> Wherein the Graver had a strife
>   With Nature, to out-do the life:
> O, could he but have drawn his wit
>   As well in brass, as he hath hit
> His face, the Print would then surpass
>   All that was ever writ in brass.
> But, since he cannot, Reader, look
>   Not on his Picture, but his Book.

The book was entitled *Mr. William Shakespeare's Comedies, Histories, & Tragedies.* Of the poems in this section, the second, third, fourth, and fifth appeared in it. The most important, of course, is also by Jonson, and is unquestionably the greatest tribute ever paid by one major writer to another, at least in English. Digges' poem has an importance of its own: it refers both to the publication of the First Folio and to the bust of Shakespeare placed on the chancel wall of Holy Trinity Church, Stratford, the same year. That he knew whom he was honoring is further borne out by the fact that his mother became the third wife of Thomas Russell, an overseer of Shakespeare's will.

The poem signed "I. M." (*I* standing for *J* in that period) has been thought by some to have been written by John Milton; but Milton was only eight when Shakespeare died in 1616, and only fifteen when the First Folio appeared. Nevertheless, the poem wears a very youthful air, and Milton could have written it; his unquestioned poem to Shakespeare was written in 1630, when he was twenty-two. Hugh Holland's sonnet concludes the Folio garland of praise. The poem by William Basse did not appear with the others, but I have placed it before Jonson's because it precedes his in time and was a point of departure for the longer, greater work.

Jonson lived to 1637 and thus was witness to the rise of a number of new writers. In his recognition and encouragement of their different qualities he demonstrated what he believed: "To judge of poets is only the faculty of poets; and not of all poets, but the best" (*Timber: or*

Discoveries). One of those "sealed of the tribe of Ben" was Thomas Randolph, who acknowledged the honor in his poem "To Ben Jonson":

> I was not born to Helicon, nor dare
> Presume to think myself a Muse's heir;
> I have no title to Parnassus Hill
> Nor any acre of it by the will
> Of a dead ancestor, nor could I be
> Ought but a tenant unto poetry;
> But thy adoption quits me of all fear,
> And makes me challenge a child's portion there.
> I am akin to heroes, being thine,
> And part of my alliance is divine:
> Orpheus, Musaeus, Homer too, beside
> Thy brothers by the Roman mother's side,
> As Ovid, Virgil, and the Latin lyre
> That is so like thee, Horace. The whole choir
> Of poets are, by thy adoption, all
> My uncles; thou hast given me power to call
> Phoebus himself my grandsire; by this grant
> Each sister of the Nine is made my aunt. . . .

(See, also, his poem in Section 9.) Another "son" was Robert Herrick, who has transmitted some of the fine frenzy of those meetings between the great figure from the age of Elizabeth and the younger poets:

> Ah Ben!
> Say how or when
> Shall we thy guests
> Meet at those lyric feasts
> Made at the *Sun*,
> The *Dog*, the *Triple Tun?*
> Where we such clusters had
> As made us nobly wild, not mad;
> And yet each verse of thine
> Outdid the meat, outdid the frolic wine.

Thomas Heywood, incidentally, has a rhymed catalogue of London taverns, which goes in part:

> The gentry to the *King's Head*,
> The nobles to the *Crown*,
> The knights unto the *Golden Fleece*,
> And to the *Plough* the clown.
> The churchman to the *Mitre*,
> The shepherd to the *Star*,

The gardener hies him to the *Rose,*
To the *Drum* the man of war.

And from the most famous tavern poem of them all, "Mr. Francis Beaumont's Letter to Ben Jonson":

> What things have we seen
> Done at the *Mermaid!* Heard words that have been
> So nimble and so full of subtle flame
> As if that everyone from whence they came
> Had meant to put his whole wit in a jest,
> And had resolved to live a fool the rest
> Of his dull life.

To conclude:

> Who shall doubt, Donne, whether I a poet be,
> When I dare send my *Epigrams* to thee,
> That so alone canst judge, so alone dost make;
> And in thy censures evenly dost take
> As free simplicity to disavow
> As thou hast best authority t'allow?
> Read all I send, and if I find but one
> Marked by thy hand, and with the better stone,
> My title's sealed. Those that for claps do write,
> Let puisnees', porters', players' praise delight,
> And, till they burst, their backs like asses load:
> A man should seek great glory, and not broad

—Ben Jonson to John Donne, with a book.

> make: from maker, poet
> stone: (*a*) in seal ring, but probably (*b*) a Roman
> allusion, to mark with a white stone—record as a
> joyful day
> puisnees: from puisne, puny or callow (youths)
> or (legal) inferior judge

The text of the sonnets is from the Oxford University Press edition of Shakespeare's *Works,* edited by W. J. Craig. Wordsworth's commentary seems closer to the truth than Browning's. Another Victorian, Matthew Arnold, saw Shakespeare plain; it is a question whether his, or Jonson's, be the greater tribute.

5.

'Come Live with Me...'

5. 'COME LIVE WITH ME...'

THE HAPPY SHEPHERDESS

I came on a happy shepherdess
   Keeping her lambs.
'God save you, rosy shepherdess!
   I am amazed to find you alone.
I will give you a dress,
   If you will take it,
All trimmed with silver thread.'

'Good-bye, knight, go your way,
   I hear my father calling me.'

PROVENÇAL SONG

OFFERINGS

I will give you painted shoes,
Fair striped kirtles,
Caps as large
As I can find.

I will give you yellow ribbons,
Shoes, sandals, slippers;
I will bring you a thousand marvels
So there won't be your peer in the village.

I will give you good gowns,
Belts and girdles,
So that amongst all the young girls
There will be none to equal you.

I will give you cheese and butter
Which I have from my flock;
I will make gittern-music
For you to go dancing.

RODRIGO DE REINOSA

THE PASSIONATE SHEPHERD TO HIS LOVE

Come live with me, and be my love,
And we will all the pleasures prove,
That valleys, groves, hills and fields,
Woods, or steepy mountain yields.

And we will sit upon the rocks,
Seeing the shepherds feed their flocks,
By shallow rivers, to whose falls
Melodious birds sing madrigals.

And I will make thee beds of roses,
And a thousand fragrant posies,
A cap of flowers, and a kirtle
Embroidered all with leaves of myrtle.

A gown made of the finest wool,
Which from our pretty lambs we pull,
Fair-linèd slippers for the cold,
With buckles of the purest gold.

A belt of straw and ivy buds,
With coral clasps and amber studs;
And if these pleasures may thee move,
Come live with me, and be my love.

The shepherd's swains shall dance and sing
For thy delight each May-morning;

If these delights thy mind may move,
Then live with me, and be my love.

CHRISTOPHER MARLOWE

THE NYMPH'S REPLY TO THE SHEPHERD

If all the world and love were young,
And truth in every shepherd's tongue,
These pretty pleasures might me move
To live with thee, and be thy love.

Time drives the flocks from field to fold,
When rivers rage and rocks grow cold,
And Philomel becometh dumb;
The rest complains of cares to come.

The flowers do fade, and wanton fields
To wayward winter reckoning yields;
A honey tongue, a heart of gall,
Is fancy's spring, but sorrow's fall.

Thy gowns, thy shoes, thy beds of roses,
Thy cap, thy kirtle, and thy posies,
Soon break, soon wither, soon forgotten:
In folly ripe, in reason rotten.

Thy belt of straw and ivy buds,
Thy coral clasps and amber studs,
All these in me no means can move
To come to thee, and be thy love.

But could youth last, and love still breed,
Had joys no date, nor age no need,
Then these delights my mind might move
To live with thee, and be thy love.

SIR WALTER RALEIGH

Philomel: the nightingale

ANOTHER OF THE SAME NATURE,
MADE SINCE

Come live with me, and be my dear,
And we will revel all the year,
In plains and groves, on hills and dales,
Where fragrant air breeds sweetest gales.

There shall you have the beauteous pine,
The cedar, and the spreading vine,
And all the woods to be a screen,
Lest Phoebus kiss my summer's queen.

The seat for your disport shall be
Over some river in a tree,
Where silver sands and pebbles sing
Eternal ditties with the spring.

There shall you see the nymphs at play,
And how the satyrs spend the day,
The fishes gliding on the sands,
Offering their bellies to your hands.

The birds with heavenly tunèd throats
Possess wood's echoes with sweet notes,
Which to your senses will impart
A music to inflame the heart.

Upon the bare and leafless oak
The ring-doves' wooings will provoke
A colder blood than you possess
To play with me, and do no less.

In bowers of laurel trimly dight
We will outwear the silent night,
While Flora busy is to spread
Her richest treasure on our bed.

Ten thousand glowworms shall attend,
And all their sparkling lights shall spend,
All to adorn and beautify
Your lodging with most majesty.

Then in mine arms will I enclose
Lily's fair mixture with the rose,
Whose nice perfections in love's play
Shall tune me to the highest key.

Thus as we pass the welcome night,
In sportful pleasures and delight,
The nimble fairies on the grounds
Shall dance and sing melodious sounds.

If these may serve for to entice
Your presence in Love's Paradise,
Then come with me, and be my dear,
And we will straight begin the year.

IGNOTO

dight: arrayed
Flora: goddess of flowers

THE BAIT

Come live with me, and be my love,
And we will some new pleasure prove
Of golden sands, and crystal brooks,
With silken lines, and silver hooks.

There will the river whispering run,
Warmed by thy eyes more than the sun,
And there th' inamored fish will stay,
Begging themselves they may betray.

When thou wilt swim in that live bath,
Each fish, which every channel hath,
Will amorously to thee swim,
Gladder to catch thee than thou him.

If thou, to be so seen, beest loath,
By sun, or moon, thou dark'nest both,
And if myself have leave to see,
I need not their light, having thee.

Let others freeze with angling reeds,
And cut their legs with shells and weeds,
Or treacherously poor fish beset
With strangling snare or windowy net.

Let coarse bold hands from slimy nest
The bedded fish in banks out-wrest,
Or curious traitors, sleave-silk flies,
Bewitch poor fishes' wand'ring eyes.

For thee, thou need'st no such deceit,
For thou thyself art thine own bait;
That fish that is not catched thereby,
Alas, is wiser far than I.

JOHN DONNE

THE RIVER GOD TO AMORET

I am this fountain's god. Below
My waters to a river grow,
And 'twixt two banks with osiers set,
That only prosper in the wet,
Through the meadows do they glide,

Wheeling still on every side,
Sometime winding round about
To find the evenest channel out.
And if thou wilt go with me,
Leaving mortal company,
In the cool streams shalt thou lie,
Free from harm as well as I;
I will give thee for thy food
No fish that useth in the mud,
But trout and pike, that love to swim
Where the gravel from the brim
Through the pure streams may be seen;
Orient pearls fit for a queen
Will I give, thy love to win,
And a shell to keep them in;
Not a fish in all my brook
That shall disobey thy look,
But, when thou wilt, come gliding by
And from thy white hand take a fly:
And to make thee understand
How I can my waves command,
They shall bubble whilst I sing,
Sweeter than the silver string.

THE SONG

Do not fear to put thy feet
Naked in the river, sweet;
Think not leech or newt or toad
Will bite thy foot, when thou hast trod;
Nor let the water rising high
As thou wad'st in, make thee cry
And sob; but ever live with me,
And not a wave shall trouble thee!

JOHN FLETCHER

AFTER CATULLUS: SONG, TO CELIA

Come, my Celia, let us prove
While we may, the sports of love;
Time will not be ours forever:
He, at length, our good will sever.
Spend not then his gifts in vain;
Suns that set may rise again,
But if once we lose this light,
'Tis with us perpetual night.
Why should we defer our joys?
Fame and rumor are but toys;
Cannot we delude the eyes
Of a few poor household spies,
Or his easier ears beguile,
So removèd by our wile?
'Tis no sin love's fruit to steal,
But the sweet theft to reveal:
To be taken, to be seen,
These have crimes accounted been.

BEN JONSON

his easier ears beguile: the husband's,
I fear

TO PHYLLIS, TO LOVE AND LIVE WITH HIM

Live, live with me, and thou shalt see
The pleasures I'll prepare for thee:
What sweets the country can afford
Shall bless thy bed and bless thy board.
The soft, sweet moss shall be thy bed,
With crawling woodbine overspread,
By which the silver-shedding streams

Shall gently melt thee into dreams.
Thy clothing, next, shall be a gown
Made of the fleece's purest down.
The tongues of kids shall be thy meat,
Their milk thy drink; and thou shalt eat
The paste of filberts for thy bread
With cream of cowslips butterèd.
Thy feasting-tables shall be hills
With daisies spread and daffodils,
Where thou shalt sit, and redbreast by,
For meat, shall give thee melody.

I'll give thee chains and carcanets
Of primroses and violets;
A bag and bottle shalt thou have—
That richly wrought, and this as brave,
So that as either shall express
The wearer's no mean shepherdess.
At shearing-times and yearly wakes,
When Themilis his pastime makes,
There thou shalt be, and be the wit—
Nay, more—the feast and grace of it.
On holidays, when virgins meet
To dance the hays with nimble feet,
Thou shalt come forth, and then appear
The Queen of Roses for that year,
And having danced ('bove all the best)
Carry the garland from the rest.
In wicker baskets maids shall bring
To thee, my dearest shepharling,
The blushing apple, bashful pear,
And shame-faced plum, all simp'ring there.
Walk in the groves, and thou shalt find
The name of Phyllis in the rind
Of every straight and smooth-skin tree,
Where kissing that, I'll twice kiss thee.
To thee a sheep-hook I will send,

Be-prinked with ribbands, to this end,
This, this alluring hook might be
Less for to catch a sheep than me.
Thou shalt have possets, wassails fine,
Not made of ale, but spicèd wine,
To make thy maids and self free mirth,
All sitting near the glitt'ring hearth.
Thou shalt have ribbands, roses, rings,
Gloves, garters, stockings, shoes, and strings
Of winning colors, that shall move
Others to lust, but me to love.
These—nay, and more—thine own shall be,
If thou wilt love, and live with me.

ROBERT HERRICK

❧ ❦

AN INVITATION TO PHYLLIS

Come live with me and be my love,
And thou shalt all the pleasures prove
The mountains' tow'ring tops can show,
Inhabiting the vales below.
From a brave height my star shall shine
T'illuminate the desert clime;
Thy summer's bower shall overlook
The subtle windings of the brook,
For thy delight, which only springs
And cuts her way with turtle's wings.
The pavement of thy rooms shall shine
With the bruised treasure of the mine,
And not a tale of love but shall
In miniature adorn thy wall.
Thy closet shall queens' caskets mock,
With rustic jewel of the rock,
And thine own light shall make a gem

As bright as these, as queens of them.
From this thy sphere thou shalt behold
Thy snowy ewes troop o'er the mold,
Who yearly pay my love a piece
Of tender lamb and silver fleece.
And when Sol's rays shall [all] combine
Thine to outburn, though not outshine,
Then at the foot of some green hill,
Where crystal Dove runs murmuring still,
We'll angle for the bright-eyed fish
To make my love a dainty dish,
Or in a cave, by Nature made,
Fly to the covert of the shade,
Where all the pleasures we will prove,
Taught by the little god of love.

   And when bright Phoebus' scorching beams
Shall cease to gild the silver streams,
Then in the cold arms of the flood
We'll bathing cool the factious blood.
Thy beauteous limbs the brook shall grace,
Like the reflex of Cynthia's face,
Whilst all the wond'ring fry do greet
The welcome light, adore thy feet,
Supposing Venus to be come
To send a kiss to Thetis home;
And following night shall trifled be,
Sweet, as thou know'st I promised thee.
Thus shall the summer's days and nights
Be dedicate to thy delights;
Then live with me, and be my love,
And all these pleasures shalt thou prove.

   But when the sapless season brings
Cold winter on her shivering wings,
Freezing the river's liquid face,
Into a crystal looking-glass,
And that the trees their naked bones

Together knock, like skeletons,
Then with the softest, whitest locks,
Spun with the tribute of thy flocks,
We will o'ercast thy whiter skin,
Winter without, a spring within.
At the first peep of day I'll rise
To make the sullen hare thy prize,
And thou with open arms shalt come
To bid the hunter welcome home.
The partridge, plover, and the poot
I'll with the subtle mallard shoot;
The fellfare, and the greedy thrush,
Shall drop from every hawthorn bush,
And the slow heron down shall fall
To feed my fairest fair withal;
The feathered people of the air
Shall fall to be my Phyllis' fare;
No storm shall touch thee, tempest move—
Then live with me, and be my love.

But from her cloister when I bring
My Phyllis to restore the spring,
The ruffling Boreas shall withdraw,
The snow shall melt, the ice shall thaw;
The agueish plants fresh leaves shall shew,
The earth put on her verdant hue,
And thou, fair Phyllis, shalt be seen
Mine, and the summer's beauteous Queen.
These, and more pleasures shalt thou prove—
Then live with me, and be my love.

CHARLES COTTON

turtle's wings: the wings of the dove
Dove: the river of that name
Cynthia: the moon goddess
Thetis: a sea goddess
poot: powt, a young partridge
fellfare: fieldfare, a thrush that winters in Britain

COME LIVE WITH ME AND BE MY LOVE

Come, live with me and be my love,
And we will all the pleasures prove
Of peace and plenty, bed and board,
That chance employment may afford.

I'll handle dainties on the docks
And thou shalt read of summer frocks:
At evening by the sour canals
We'll hope to hear some madrigals.

Care on thy maiden brow shall put
A wreath of wrinkles, and thy foot
Be shod with pain: not silken dress
But toil shall tire thy loveliness.

Hunger shall make thy modest zone
And cheat fond death of all but bone—
If these delights thy mind may move,
Then live with me and be my love.

C. DAY LEWIS

tire: attire
zone: belt or girdle

⤳ *NOTES* ⤶

The Provençal song dates from the thirteenth century, the Spanish pastoral from the fifteenth. Both were called to my attention by Willard Trask, who translated them for my use.

The Marlowe and Raleigh poems were immensely popular. Both can be seen, in parallel columns on a black-letter broadside decorated with woodcuts of an Elizabethan lady and gentleman who are very much beplumed and beruffed; the lady holds a flower. "A most excellent Ditty of the Lover's promises to his beloved," says the heading over Marlowe's poem, adding, "To a sweet new tune called, *Live with me and be my love.*" One of those who sang it was John Taylor, the "Water-Poet," as he sculled passengers across the Thames; he was also a deep-sea sailor and took part in the siege of Cadiz under the Earl of Essex. Raleigh's poem is headed "The Lady's prudent answer to her Love. To the same tune." In Act III, Scene 1, of *The Merry Wives of Windsor,* the last two lines of Marlowe's second stanza and the first two lines of the third stanza are sung by Hugh Evans, perhaps to the sweet new tune. And in *As You Like It,* Shakespeare alludes to Marlowe's title, although the "saw" he quotes is from *Hero and Leander:*

> Dead shepherd, now I find thy saw of might:
> 'Who ever lov'd that lov'd not at first sight?'

The versions I have given of Marlowe's and Raleigh's poems are from *England's Helicon,* 1600; the first is signed *"Chr. Marlow,"* but Raleigh's bears the signature "Ignoto." A second *Ignoto* poem follows; but whoever this poet was, he remains precisely what he termed himself or was termed by the editor of the anthology: unknown.

Another anonymous poem in *England's Helicon* provides a variation on the theme; in it, the shepherd and his love offer each other gifts. It is in the form of a dialogue, entitled "Phyllida's Love-Call to her Corydon, and His Replying." Two of its stanzas follow:

> PHYLLIDA
> Here are cherries ripe, my Corydon,
> Eat them for my sake.

> CORYDON
> Here's my oaten pipe, my lovely one,
> Sport for thee to make.

PHYLLIDA
Here are threads, my true love, fine as silk,
To knit thee, to knit thee
A pair of stockings white as milk.

CORYDON
Here are reeds, my true love, fine and neat,
To make thee, to make thee
A bonnet to withstand the heat.

PHYLLIDA
I will gather flowers, my Corydon
To set in thy cap.

CORYDON
I will gather pearls, my lovely one,
To put in thy lap.

PHYLLIDA
I will buy my true love garters gay
For Sundays, for Sundays,
To wear about his legs so tall.

CORYDON
I will buy my true love yellow say
For Sundays, for Sundays,
To wear about her middle small.

say: fine cloth, serge

John Donne, who also served under Essex at the siege of Cadiz, appears to have read and relished Ignoto II's poem, for he has taken his chief theme from it.

Izaak Walton wrote in *The Compleat Angler* (1653):

Her voice was good, and the ditty fitted for it; 'twas that smooth song which was made by Kit Marlowe, now at least fifty years ago: and the milkmaid's mother sung an answer to it, which was made by Sir Walter Raleigh in his younger days. They were old fashioned poetry, but choicely good, I think much better than the strong lines that are now in fashion in this critical age.

Of Donne's poem, he wrote that it was "made to show the world that he could make soft and smooth verses when he thought smoothness worth his labor; and I love them the better because they allude to rivers, and fish and fishing."

Donne was followed by Herrick and Cotton, who appear to have been unable to stop, once started on their imitations. Cotton, who wrote the second part of *The Compleat Angler* ("how to angle for a Trout or Grayling in a clear stream"), was an outdoors man, and is more specific about the pleasures the country can afford.

Fletcher's "The River God to Amoret" is from *The Faithful Shepherdess;* Jonson's "Song" (which, as indicated, draws heavily on Catullus) is from *Volpone.*

It remained for a modern poet, C. Day Lewis, to transform the pastoral into an industrial setting, and to make his poem a vehicle of social protest. His "Come, live with me" is the second of "Two songs" in *A Time To Dance,* 1936; the first, beginning "I've heard them lilting at loom and belting," is a proletarian version of "I've heard them lilting at our ewe-milking," from "A Lament for Flodden" by Jane Elliot, 1727–1805.

Lewis and Raleigh aside, it remains to be asked what happens when the gifts proffered are received. The answer is doleful, and to the tune of "Greensleeves." "A New Courtly Sonnet of the Lady Greensleeves" was registered in 1580 and appeared in *A Handful of Pleasant Delights,* 1584. Some of its stanzas follow:

> I bought thee kerchiefs for thy head,
> That were wrought fine and gallantly;
> I kept thee both at board and bed,
> Which cost my purse well-favoredly.

> I bought thee petticoats of the best,
> The cloth so fine as fine might be;
> I gave thee jewels for thy chest,
> And all this cost I spent on thee.

> Thy smock of silk, both fair and white,
> With gold embroidered gorgeously;
> Thy petticoat of sendal right,
> And thus I bought thee gladly.

> Thy girdle of gold so red,
> With pearls bedecked sumptuously,
> The like no other lasses had,
> And yet thou wouldst not love me.

> well-favoredly: plenty
> sendal: thin silk

6.

A Shropshire Medley

6. A SHROPSHIRE MEDLEY

O MISTRESS MINE
WHERE ARE YOU ROAMING?

O mistress mine! where are you roaming?
O! stay and hear; your true love's coming,
   That can sing both high and low.
Trip no further, pretty sweeting;
Journeys end in lovers meeting,
   Every wise man's son doth know.

What is love? 'tis not hereafter;
Present mirth hath present laughter;
   What's to come is still unsure:
In delay there lies no plenty;
Then come kiss me, sweet and twenty,
   Youth's a stuff will not endure.

WILLIAM SHAKESPEARE

SONG

Pluck the fruit and taste the pleasure,
   Youthful lordings, of delight;
Whilst occasion gives you seizure,
   Feed your fancies and your sight:

After death, when you are gone,
Joy and pleasure is there none.

Here on earth nothing is stable,
  Fortune's changes well are known;
Whilst as youth doth then enable,
  Let your seeds of joy be sown:
    After death, when you are gone,
    Joy and pleasure is there none.

Feast it freely with your lovers,
  Blithe and wanton sweets do fade;
Whilst that lovely Cupid hovers
  Round about this lonely shade,
    Sport it freely, one to one;
    After death is pleasure none.

Now the pleasant spring allureth,
  And both place and time invites;
Out, alas! what heart endureth
  To disclaim his sweet delights?
    After death, when we are gone,
    Joy and pleasure is there none.

THOMAS LODGE

LONG-EXPECTED ONE-AND-TWENTY

Long-expected one-and-twenty,
  Ling'ring year, at length is flown;
Pride and pleasure, pomp and plenty,
  Great Sir John, are now your own.

Loosen'd from the minor's tether,
  Free to mortgage or to sell,
Wild as wind, and light as feather,
  Bid the sons of thrift farewell.

Call the Betseys, Kates and Jennies,
    All the names that banish care;
Lavish of your grandsire's guineas,
    Show the spirit of an heir.

All that prey on vice or folly
    Joy to see their quarry fly;
There the gamester, light and jolly,
    There the lender, grave and sly.

Wealth, my lad, was made to wander,
    Let it wander as it will;
Call the jockey, call the pander,
    Bid them come and take their fill.

When the bonny blade carouses,
    Pockets full, and spirits high—
What are acres? what are houses?
    Only dirt, or wet or dry.

Should the guardian friend or mother
    Tell the woes of wilful waste;
Scorn their counsel, scorn their pother,—
    You can hang or drown at last.

SAMUEL JOHNSON

TO [MISS BLACKETT]

On Her First Ascent to the Summit of Helvellyn

Inmate of a mountain-dwelling,
Thou hast clomb aloft, and gazed
From the watch-towers of Helvellyn;
Awed, delighted, and amazed!

Potent was the spell that bound thee
Not unwilling to obey;

For blue Ether's arms, flung round thee,
Stilled the pantings of dismay.

Lo! the dwindled woods and meadows;
What a vast abyss is there!
Lo! the clouds, the solemn shadows,
And the glistenings—heavenly fair!

And a record of commotion
Which a thousand ridges yield;
Ridge, and gulf, and distant ocean
Gleaming like a silver shield!

Now—take flight;—possess, inherit
Alps or Andes—they are thine!
With the morning's roseate Spirit,
Sweep their length of snowy line;

Or survey their bright dominions
In the gorgeous colors drest
Flung from off the purple pinions,
Evening spreads throughout the west!

Thine are all the coral fountains
Warbling in each sparry vault
Of the untrodden lunar mountains;
Listen to their songs!—or halt,

To Niphates' top invited,
Whither spiteful Satan steered;
Or descend where the ark alighted,
When the green earth re-appeared;

For the power of the hills is on thee,
As was witnessed through thine eye
Then when old Helvellyn won thee
To confess their majesty!

WILLIAM WORDSWORTH

REVEILLE

Wake: the silver dusk returning
    Up the beach of darkness brims,
And the ship of sunrise burning
    Strands upon the eastern rims.

Wake: the vaulted shadow shatters
    Trampled to the floor it spanned,
And the tent of night in tatters
    Straws the sky-pavilioned land.

Up, lad, up, 'tis late for lying:
    Hear the drums of morning play;
Hark, the empty highways crying
    'Who'll beyond the hills away?'

Towns and countries woo together,
    Forelands beacon, belfries call;
Never lad that trod on leather
    Lived to feast his heart with all.

Up, lad: thews that lie and cumber
    Sunlit pallets never thrive;
Morns abed and daylight slumber
    Were not meant for man alive.

Clay lies still, but blood's a rover;
    Breath's a ware that will not keep.
Up, lad: when the journey's over
    There'll be time enough to sleep.

A. E. HOUSMAN

A LOVE SONNET

I loved a lass, a fair one,
    As fair as e'er was seen;
She was indeed a rare one,
    Another Sheba Queen:

But, fool as then I was,
    I thought she loved me too:
But now, alas! sh'as left me,
    Falero, lero, loo!

Her hair like gold did glister,
    Each eye was like a star,
She did surpass her sister,
    Which passed all others far;
She would me honey call,
    She'd—oh, she'd kiss me too!
But now, alas! sh'as left me,
    Falero, lero, loo!

In summer time to Medley
    My love and I would go:
The boatmen there stood read'ly
    My love and me to row;
For cream there would we call,
    For cakes and for prunes too:
But now, alas! sh'as left me,
    Falero, lero, loo!

Many a merry meeting
    My love and I have had;
She was my only sweeting,
    She made my heart full glad;
The tears stood in her eyes
    Like to the morning dew:
But now, alas! sh'as left me,
    Falero, lero, loo!

And as abroad we walkèd,
    As lovers' fashion is,
Oft as we sweetly talkèd
    The sun would steal a kiss;
The wind upon her lips
    Likewise most sweetly blew:

But now, alas! sh'as left me,
  Falero, lero, loo!

Her cheeks were like the cherry,
    Her skin was white as snow;
When she was blithe and merry
    She angel-like did show;
Her waist exceeding small,
    The fives did fit her shoe:
But now, alas! sh'as left me,
    Falero, lero, loo!

In summer time or winter
    She had her heart's desire;
I still did scorn to stint her
    From sugar, sack, or fire:
The world went round about,
    No cares we ever knew:
But now, alas! sh'as left me,
    Falero, lero, loo!

As we walked home together,
    At midnight, through the town,
To keep away the weather
    O'er her I'd cast my gown;
No cold my love should feel,
    Whate'er the heavens could do:
But now, alas! sh'as left me,
    Falero, lero, loo!

Like doves we would be billing,
    And clip and kiss so fast,
Yet she would be unwilling
    That I should kiss the last:
They're Judas kisses now,
    Since that they proved untrue:
For now, alas! sh'as left me,
    Falero, lero, loo!

To maidens' vows and swearing
   Henceforth no credit give;
You may give them the hearing,
   But never them believe;
They are as false as fair,
   Unconstant, frail, untrue:
For mine, alas! has left me,
   Falero, lero, loo!

'Twas I that paid for all things,
   'Twas others drank the wine;
I cannot now recall things,
   Live but a fool to pine;
'Twas I that beat the bush,
   The bird to others flew:
For she, alas, hath left me,
   Falero, lero, loo!

If ever that Dame Nature,
   For this false lover's sake,
Another pleasing creature
   Like unto her would make,
Let her remember this—
   To make the other true:
For this, alas! hath left me,
   Falero, lero, loo!

No riches now can raise me,
   No want make me despair,
No misery amaze me,
   Nor yet for want I care;
I have lost a world itself:
   My earthly heaven, adieu!
Since she, alas! hath left me,
   Falero, lero, loo!

GEORGE WITHER

sack: sherry

BREDON HILL

In summertime on Bredon
   The bells they sound so clear;
Round both the shires they ring them
   In steeples far and near,
   A happy noise to hear.

Here of a Sunday morning
   My love and I would lie,
And see the colored counties,
   And hear the larks so high
   About us in the sky.

The bells would ring to call her
   In valleys miles away:
'Come all to church, good people;
   Good people, come and pray.'
   But here my love would stay.

And I would turn and answer
   Among the springing thyme,
'Oh, peal upon our wedding,
   And we will hear the chime,
   And come to church in time.'

But when the snows at Christmas
   On Bredon top were strown,
My love rose up so early
   And stole out unbeknown
   And went to church alone.

They tolled the one bell only,
   Groom there was none to see,
The mourners followed after,
   And so to church went she,
   And would not wait for me.

The bells they sound on Bredon,
   And still the steeples hum.

'Come all to church, good people,'—
Oh, noisy bells, be dumb;
I hear you, I will come.

A. E. HOUSMAN

THE THREE ROSES

When the buds began to burst,
Long ago, with Rose the First
I was walking; joyous then,
Far above all other men,
Till before us up there stood
Britonferry's oaken wood,
Whispering, *Happy as thou art,*
Happiness and thou must part.
Many summers have gone by
Since a second Rose and I
(Rose from that same stem) have told
This and other tales of old.
She upon her wedding-day
Carried home my tenderest lay;
From her lap I now have heard
Gleeful chirping, Rose the Third.
Not for *her* this hand of mine
Rhyme with nuptial wreath shall twine;
Cold and torpid it must lie,
Mute the tongue, and closed the eye.

WALTER SAVAGE LANDOR

ALONG THE FIELD AS WE CAME BY

Along the field as we came by
A year ago, my love and I,
The aspen over stile and stone
Was talking to itself alone.

'Oh who are these that kiss and pass?
A country lover and his lass;
Two lovers looking to be wed;
And time shall put them both to bed,
But she shall lie with earth above,
And he beside another love.'

And sure enough beneath the tree
There walks another love with me,
And overhead the aspen heaves
Its rainy-sounding silver leaves;
And I spell nothing in their stir,
But now perhaps they speak to her,
And plain for her to understand
They talk about a time at hand
When I shall sleep with clover clad,
And she beside another lad.

A. E. HOUSMAN

IT WAS A LOVER AND HIS LASS

It was a lover and his lass,
   With a hey, and a ho, and a hey nonino,
That o'er the green corn-field did pass,
   In the spring time, the only pretty ring time,
When birds do sing, hey ding a ding, ding;
Sweet lovers love the spring.

Between the acres of the rye,
   With a hey, and a ho, and a hey nonino,
These pretty country folks would lie,
   In the spring time, &c.

This carol they began that hour,
   With a hey, and a ho, and a hey nonino,
How that a life was but a flower
   In the spring time, &c.

And therefore take the present time,
    With a hey, and a ho, and a hey nonino;
For love is crownèd with the prime
    In the spring time, *&c.*

WILLIAM SHAKESPEARE

WINTER: AN ODE

No more the morn, with tepid rays,
    Unfolds the flower of various hue;
Noon spreads no more the genial blaze,
    Nor gentle eve distils the dew.
The ling'ring hours prolong the night,
    Usurping darkness shares the day;
Her mists restrain the force of light,
    And Phoebus holds a doubtful sway.
By gloomy twilight half reveal'd,
    With sighs we view the hoary hill,
The leafless wood, the naked field,
    The snow-topped cot, the frozen rill.
No music warbles through the grove,
    No vivid colors paint the plain;
No more with devious steps I rove
    Through verdant paths, now sought in vain.
Aloud the driving tempest roars,
    Congeal'd, impetuous showers descend;
Haste, close the window, bar the doors,
    Fate leaves me Stella, and a friend.
In nature's aid, let art supply
    With light and heat my little sphere;
Rouse, rouse the fire, and pile it high,
    Light up a constellation here.
Let music sound the voice of joy,

Or mirth repeat the jocund tale;
Let Love his wanton wiles employ,
   And o'er the season wine prevail,
Yet time life's dreary winter brings,
   When Mirth's gay tale shall please no more;
Nor music charm—though Stella sings;
   Nor love, nor wine, the Spring restore.
Catch then, Oh! catch the transient hour,
   Improve each moment as it flies;
Life's a short summer—man a flower:
   He dies—alas! how soon he dies!

SAMUEL JOHNSON

OH SEE HOW THICK
THE GOLDCUP FLOWERS

Oh see how thick the goldcup flowers
   Are lying in field and lane,
With dandelions to tell the hours
   That never are told again.
Oh may I squire you round the meads
   And pick you posies gay?
—'Twill do no harm to take my arm.
   'You may, young man, you may.'

Ah, spring was sent for lass and lad,
   'Tis now the blood runs gold,
And man and maid had best be glad
   Before the world is old.
What flowers today may flower tomorrow,
   But never as good as new.
—Suppose I wound my arm right round—
   ' 'Tis true, young man, 'tis true.'

Some lads there are, 'tis shame to say,
   That only court to thieve,
And once they bear the bloom away
   'Tis little enough they leave.
Then keep your heart for men like me
   And safe from trustless chaps.
My love is true and all for you.
   'Perhaps, young man, perhaps.'

Oh, look in my eyes then, can you doubt?
   —Why, 'tis a mile from town.
How green the grass is all about!
   We might as well sit down.
—Ah, life, what is it but a flower?
   Why must true lovers sigh?
Be kind, have pity, my own, my pretty,—
   'Good-bye, young man, good-bye.'

A. E. HOUSMAN

≽ ≼

HORACE, BOOK IV, ODE 7

The snow dissolv'd, no more is seen,
The fields and woods, behold! are green;
The changing year renews the plain,
The rivers know their banks again;
The sprightly nymph and naked grace
The mazy dance together trace;
The changing year's successive plan
Proclaims mortality to man;
Rough winter's blasts to spring give way,
Spring yields to summer's sov'reign ray;
Then summer sinks in autumn's reign,
And winter chills the world again;
Her losses soon the moon supplies,

But wretched man, when once he lies
Where Priam and his sons are laid,
Is nought but ashes and a shade.
Who knows if Jove, who counts our score,
Will toss us in a morning more?

SAMUEL JOHNSON

ON WENLOCK EDGE
THE WOOD'S IN TROUBLE

On Wenlock Edge the wood's in trouble;
His forest fleece the Wrekin heaves;
The gale, it plies the saplings double,
And thick on Severn snow the leaves.

'Twould blow like this through holt and hanger
When Uricon the city stood:
'Tis the old wind in the old anger,
But then it threshed another wood.

Then, 'twas before my time, the Roman
At yonder heaving hill would stare:
The blood that warms an English yeoman,
The thoughts that hurt him, they were there.

There, like the wind through woods in riot,
Through him the gale of life blew high;
The tree of man was never quiet:
Then 'twas the Roman, now 'tis I.

The gale, it plies the saplings double,
It blows so hard, 'twill soon be gone:
Today the Roman and his trouble
Are ashes under Uricon.

A. E. HOUSMAN

holt: copse, underwood
hanger: wooded hillside

IMITATION IN THE STYLE OF * * * *

Hermit hoar, in solemn cell
    Wearing out life's evening grey,
Strike thy bosom, sage, and tell,
    What is bliss, and which the way?

Thus I spoke, and speaking sighed,
    Scarce repressed the starting tear,
When the hoary sage replied,
    Come, my lad, and drink some beer!

SAMUEL JOHNSON

****: [Thomas] Gray

THE CHESTNUT CASTS HIS FLAMBEAUX

The chestnut casts his flambeaux, and the flowers
    Stream from the hawthorn on the wind away,
The doors clap to, the pane is blind with showers.
    Pass me the can, lad; there's an end of May.

There's one spoilt spring to scant our mortal lot,
    One season ruined of our little store.
May will be fine next year as like as not:
    Oh ay, but then we shall be twenty-four.

We for a certainty are not the first
    Have sat in taverns while the tempest hurled
Their hopeful plans to emptiness, and cursed
    Whatever brute and blackguard made the world,

It is in truth iniquity on high
    To cheat our sentenced souls of aught they crave,
And mar the merriment as you and I
    Fare on our long fool's-errand to the grave.

Iniquity it is; but pass the can.
   My lad, no pair of kings our mothers bore;
Our only portion is the estate of man:
   We want the moon, but we shall get no more.

If here today the cloud of thunder lours
   Tomorrow it will hie on far behests;
The flesh will grieve on other bones than ours
   Soon, and the soul will mourn in other breasts.

The troubles of our proud and angry dust
   Are from eternity, and shall not fail.
Bear them we can, and if we can we must.
   Shoulder the sky, my lad, and drink your ale.

                                        A. E. HOUSMAN

❧ *NOTES* ❧

The song "O Mistress Mine!" is from *Twelfth Night,* Act II, Scene 3. Lodge's "Song" is from *Robert, Second Duke of Normandy,* 1591. Subject matter, movement, a way of phrasing, are already there, to be reinforced by Wordsworth, and Johnson, to whom I will return. Wither contributes a specific rhythm; Landor, subject matter. A word about the "three Roses."

In Swansea, Wales, about the year 1796, Landor met the Hon. Rose Whitworth Aylmer, then sixteen years old. She was the only daughter of the fourth Baron Aylmer; her mother was the daughter of Sir Charles Whitworth. The friendship that followed continued uninterrupted until 1798, when Miss Aylmer went with her aunt, Lady Russell, to Calcutta where, two years later, at the house of Sir Henry Russell, she died suddenly. In 1909, a tablet inscribed with Landor's most perfect poem was affixed to the monument over her grave. The poem exists in several versions; the best, which was chosen, appeared in the 1846 edition of Landor's *Works.* Swinburne, who was consulted, not only thought this text superior, but expressed the view that Landor would have approved of the tablet. The 1846 text follows:

> Ah what avails the sceptred race,
>   Ah what the form divine!
> What every virtue, every grace!
>   Rose Aylmer, all were thine.
> Rose Aylmer, whom these wakeful eyes
>   May weep, but never see,
> A night of memories and of sighs
>   I consecrate to thee.

This was "Rose the First." Her widowed mother married again and bore another daughter—the "second Rose"—who was the mother of "Rose the Third."

I have included "It Was a Lover and His Lass," from Act V, Scene 3 of *As You Like It,* for the flower phrase in the third stanza. It reappears in Johnson's "Winter: An Ode," which also has a prefiguring of

> The doors clap to, the pane is blind with showers

in "The Chestnut Casts His Flambeaux." But thus particularized it can be found in the first part of *Henry IV,* Act II, Scene 4:

Hostess, clap to the doors.

As for Johnson's translation from Horace, Housman also translated this ode, and its somber mood and echoes stayed with him when he wrote "On Wenlock Edge."

Housman's reading ranged far and wide. Burton's *Anatomy of Melancholy*—which was, Johnson told the Rev. Dr. Maxwell, "the only book that ever took him out of bed two hours sooner than he wished to rise"—has the following paragraph—the first—under the heading "Prognosticks of Love-Melancholy":

> What Fires, Torments, Cares, Jealousies, Suspicions, Fears, Griefs, Anxieties, accompany such as are in love, I have sufficiently said: the next question is, what will be the event of such miseries, what they foretell. Some are of opinion that this love cannot be cured, there flowers no balm to sain them, it accompanies them to the last.

> There flowers no balm to sain him
> From east of earth to west
> That's lost for everlasting
> The heart out of his breast.
> (*A Shropshire Lad,* No. XIV)

And now, credit where credit is due.

Readers familiar with Boswell's *Life* will recall the following passage, when Johnson was on his deathbed: "He repeated with great spirit a poem, consisting of several stanzas, in four lines, in alternate rhyme, which he said he had composed some years before, on the occasion of a rich, extravagant young gentleman's coming of age; saying he had never repeated it but once since he composed it, and had given but one copy of it. That copy was given to Mrs. Thrale, now Piozzi, who has published it in a Book which she entitles *British Synonymy*." The "Great Sir John" of the fourth line in the first stanza was Sir John Lade, a nephew and ward of Mr. Thrale; he came of age August 1, 1780. On August 8 Johnson sent Mrs. Thrale "a short song of congratulation, which you must not show to anybody." (She merely published it.) Johnson termed it "one of the author's first essays in that way of writing, and a beginner is always to be treated with tenderness." The only other connection Sir John had with the world of books was *The Gentleman's Stable Directory,* which was dedicated to him. He went through his guineas at a rapid rate.

I had long been aware of Johnsonian influences in Housman's work;

my essay, "Dr. Johnson and *A Shropshire Lad*" appeared in *Poetry,* August, 1942. Many years later, Dr. Herman W. Liebert, of the Editorial Committee of the Yale Editions of the Private Papers of James Boswell, called my attention to the following note by G. M. Young in *Johnson: Prose and Poetry,* Mona Wilson, editor, Harvard University Press, 1951:

"Housman was staying one week-end with W. P. Ker in All Souls. After breakfast on Sunday they were standing in the garden together. W. P. K. waved to me to join them. As I came up they were talking about Johnson's verses, and Housman said either, 'The poem started the Shropshire Lad' or (more nearly I think) 'That poem was in my mind when I was starting the Shropshire Lad.' "

The poem, of course, was "Long-Expected One-and-Twenty."

Housman had not only read Johnson's poems—he was also familiar with Boswell's *Life* and the *Journal of a Tour to the Hebrides.* In the *Life,* Boswell relates that he thought "Hermit hoar, in solemn cell" "very good solemn poetry," and after quoting its two stanzas, commented: "The advice is as good as can be given to a low-spirited, dissatisfied being:—'Don't trouble your head with sickly thinking: take a cup, and be merry.' " Housman turned this into the poem beginning, "Think no more, lad; laugh, be jolly." In the *Journal,* Johnson is quoted as saying: "Sir, sorrow is inherent in humanity. As you cannot judge two and two to be either five, or three, but certainly four, so, when comparing a worse present state with a better which is past, you cannot but feel sorrow." (There is an echo of this in the *Life*—Johnson talking to a poet who had made Genius feminine: "Sir, you are giving a reason for it; but that will not make it right. You may have a reason why two and two should make five, but they will still make but four.") The same thought, the identical numbers, reappear in Housman:

> To think that two and two are four
> And neither five nor three
> The heart of man has long been sore
> And long 'tis like to be.

The foreword to E. E. Cummings' *is 5* (1926) ends as follows:

Ineluctable preoccupation with The Verb gives a poet one priceless advantage: whereas nonmakers must content themselves with the merely undeniable fact that two times two is four, he rejoices in a purely irresistible truth (to be found, in abbreviated costume, upon the title page of the present volume).

7.

Love

7. LOVE

TO HIS BOOK (1691)

Go, little book, and to the world impart
The faithful image of an amorous heart;
Those who love's dear, deluding pains have known,
May in my fatal stories read their own;
Those who have lived from all its torments free,
May find the thing they never felt, from me;
Perhaps, advised, avoid the gilded bait,
And, warned by my example, shun my fate:
While with calm joy, safe landed on the coast,
I view the waves on which I once was toss't.
Love is a medley of endearments, jars,
Suspicions, quarrels, reconcilements, wars,
Then peace again. O would it not be best
To chase the fatal passion from our breast?
But since so few can live from passion free,
Happy the man, and only happy he,
Who with such lucky stars begins his love,
That his cool judgment does his choice approve.
Ill-grounded passions quickly wear away;
What's built upon esteem, can ne'er decay.

WILLIAM WALSH

HOW TO CHOOSE A MISTRESS

First I would have a face exactly fair,
Not long, nor yet precisely circular;
A smooth, high brow where neither age, nor yet
A froward peevishness hath wrinkles set;
And under that a pair of clear black eyes
To be the windows of the edifice,
Not sunk into her head, nor starting out,
Not fixed, nor rolling wantonly about,
But gently moving, as to whet the sight
By some fresh object, not the appetite,
Their orbs both equal, and divided by
A well-proportioned nose's ivory,
The nostrils open, fit to try what air
Would best preserve the mansion, what impair;
The color in her cheek so mixed, the eye
Cannot distinguish where the red doth lie,
Or white, but every part thereof, as loath
To yield in either, equally have both;
The mouth but little, whence proceeds a breath
Which might revive one in the gates of death,
And envy strike in the Panchayan groves
When their spiced tops a gentle east wind moves;
The lips ruddy, as blushing to be known
Kissing each other by the lookers-on,
And these not to perpetual talk disposed,
Nor always in a lumpish silence closed,
But ev'ry word her innocence brings forth,
Sweetened by a discreet and harmless mirth;
The teeth even and white; a dimpled chin;
And all these clothèd with the purest skin;
Then, as good painters ever use to place
The darker shadow to the fairer face,
A sad, brown hair, whose am'rous curls may tie
The pris'ners fast ta'en captive by her eye.
Thus would I have her face. And for her mind,

I'd have it clothed in virtue, not behind
The other's beauty; for a house thus drest
Should be provided of a noble guest.
Then would I have a body so refined
Fit to support this face, enclose this mind.
When all these graces I in one do prove,
Then may death blind me if I do not love;
Yet there is one thing more must needs concur—
She must love me as well as I love her.

EDMUND PRESTWICH

froward: perverse
Panchayan: from Panchaia,
 a part of Arabia Felix
 famous for its incense-laden trees

᚛ ᚜

SONG

Oh, how hard it is to find
The one just suited to our mind;
 And if that one should be
False, unkind, or found too late,
What can we do but sigh at fate,
 And sing *'Woe's me—Woe's me?'*

Love's a boundless burning waste,
Where bliss's stream we seldom taste,
 And still more seldom flee
Suspense's thorns, suspicion's stings;
Yet somehow love a something brings
 That's sweet—ev'n when we sigh *'Woe's me!'*

THOMAS CAMPBELL

BROWN PENNY

I whispered, 'I am too young,'
And then, 'I am old enough';
Wherefore I threw a penny
To find out if I might love.
'Go and love, go and love, young man,
If the lady be young and fair.'
Ah, penny, brown penny, brown penny,
I am looped in the loops of her hair.
O love is the crooked thing,
There is nobody wise enough
To find out all that is in it,
For he would be thinking of love
Till the stars had run away
And the shadows eaten the moon.
Ah, penny, brown penny, brown penny,
One cannot begin it too soon.

WILLIAM BUTLER YEATS

≿ ≾

A NYMPH'S PASSION

I love, and he loves me again,
    Yet dare I not tell who;
For if the nymphs should know my swain,
    I fear they'd love him, too.
        Yet if it be not known,
        The pleasure is as good as none,
For that's a narrow joy is but our own.

I'll tell, that if they be not glad,
    They yet may envy me;

But then if I grow jealous-mad,
    And of them pitied be,
        It were a plague 'bove scorn,
        And yet it cannot be forborne,
Unless my heart would as my thought be torn.

He is, if they can find him, fair,
    And fresh and fragrant, too,
As summer's sky or purgèd air,
    And looks as lilies do
        That were this morning blown;
        Yet, yet I doubt he is not known,
And fear much more, that more of him be shown.

But he hath eyes so round, and bright,
    As make away my doubt,
Where Love may all his torches light,
    Though hate had put them out;
        But then to increase my fears,
        What nymph soe'er his voice but hears
Will be my rival, though she have but ears.

I'll tell no more, and yet I love,
    And he loves me; yet no
One unbecoming thought doth move
    From either heart, I know;
        But so exempt from blame,
        As it would be to each a fame
If love, or fear, would let me tell his name.

BEN JONSON

TO CHLORIS

See, Chloris, how the clouds
Tilt in the azure lists,
And how with Stygian mists
Each hornèd hill his giant forehead shrouds;

Jove thund'reth in the air,
The air, grown great with rain,
Now seems to bring Deucalion's days again.
I see thee quake; come, let us home repair,
Come hide thee in mine arms,
If not for love, yet to shun greater harms.

WILLIAM DRUMMOND OF HAWTHORNDEN

lists: tournaments
Stygian: from Styx, dark river of Hades
Deucalion's days: the Flood

WHEN I SET OUT FOR LYONNESSE

When I set out for Lyonnesse,
    A hundred miles away,
    The rime was on the spray,
And starlight lit my lonesomeness
When I set out for Lyonnesse
    A hundred miles away.

What would bechance at Lyonnesse
    While I should sojourn there
    No prophet durst declare,
Nor did the wisest wizard guess
What would bechance at Lyonnesse
    While I should sojourn there.

When I came back from Lyonnesse
    With magic in my eyes,
    All marked with mute surmise
My radiance rare and fathomless,
When I came back from Lyonnesse
    With magic in my eyes!

THOMAS HARDY

LOVE'S HARMONY

Other slow arts entirely keep the brain,
And therefore, finding barren practisers,
Scarce show a harvest of their heavy toil;
But love, first learnèd in a lady's eyes,
Lives not alone immurèd in the brain,
But, with the motion of all elements,
Courses as swift as thought in every power,
And gives to every power a double power,
Above their functions and their offices.
It adds a precious seeing to the eye;
A lover's eyes will gaze an eagle blind;
A lover's ear will hear the lowest sound,
When the suspicious head of theft is stopp'd;
Love's feeling is more soft and sensible
Than are the tender horns of cockled snails;
Love's tongue proves dainty Bacchus gross in taste.
For valor, is not love a Hercules,
Still climbing trees in the Hesperides?
Subtle as sphinx; as sweet and musical
As bright Apollo's lute, strung with his hair;
And when love speaks, the voice of all the gods
Makes heaven drowsy with the harmony.

WILLIAM SHAKESPEARE

Hercules: he stole the golden apples of the Hesperides,
but without climbing trees—he merely held up the
heavens while Atlas fetched them for him

LOVE'S LABOUR LOST

Love's Labour Lost, I once did see a play
Yclepèd so, so callèd to my pain,
Which I to hear to my small joy did stay,

Giving attendance on my froward dame;
  My misgiving mind presaging to me ill,
  Yet was I drawn to see it 'gainst my will.

This play, no play but plague was unto me,
For there I lost the love I likèd most:
And what to others seemed a jest to be,
I that in earnest found unto my cost:
  To every one save me 'twas comical,
  Whilst tragic-like to me it did befall.

Each actor played in cunning-wise his part,
But chiefly those entrapped in Cupid's snare:
Yet all was feignèd, 'twas not from the heart,
They seemed to grieve, but yet they felt no care;
  'Twas I that grief indeed did bear in breast,
  The others did but make a show in jest.

Yet neither feigning theirs, nor my mere truth,
Could make her once so much as for to smile:
Whilst she, despite of pity mild and ruth,
Did sit as scorning of my woes the while.
  Thus did she sit to see Love lose his love,
  Like hardened rock that force nor power can move.

ROBERT TOFTE

Yclepèd: called
ruth: compassion

NEVER SEEK TO TELL THY LOVE

Never seek to tell thy love,
  Love that never told can be;
For the gentle wind doth move
  Silently, invisibly.

I told my love, I told my love,
  I told her all my heart,
Trembling, cold, in ghastly fears,
  Ah! she did depart!

Soon after she was gone from me,
   A traveller came by,
Silently, invisibly:
   He took her with a sigh.

WILLIAM BLAKE

SECRET LOVE

I hid my love when young till I
Couldn't bear the buzzing of a fly;
I hid my life to my despite
Till I could not bear to look at light:
I dare not gaze upon her face
But left her memory in each place;
Where'er I saw a wild flower lie
I kissed and bade my love good-bye.

I met her in the greenest dells,
Where dewdrops pearl the wood bluebells;
The lost breeze kissed her bright blue eye,
The bee kissed and went singing by,
A sunbeam found a passage there,
A gold chain round her neck so fair;
As secret as the wild bee's song
She lay there all the summer long.

I hid my love in field and town
Till e'en the breeze would knock me down;
The bees seemed singing ballads o'er,
The fly's bass turned a lion's roar;
And even silence found a tongue,
To haunt me all the summer long;
The riddle nature could not prove
Was nothing else but secret love.

JOHN CLARE

MERCILESS BEAUTY: A TRIPLE RONDEL

I

Captivity

Your eyen two will slay me suddenly,
I may the beauty of them not sustain,
So woundeth it throughout my heart keen.

And but your word will healen hastily
My heart's wound, while that it is green,
 Your eyen two will slay me suddenly,
 I may the beauty of them not sustain.

Upon my troth I say you faithfully,
That you been of my life and death the queen;
For with my death the truth shall be seen.
 Your eyen two will slay me suddenly,
 I may the beauty of them not sustain,
 So woundeth it throughout my heart keen.

II

Rejection

So hath your beauty from your heart chased
Pity, that me availeth not to plain;
For danger holds your mercy in his chain.

Guiltless my death thus have you me purchased;
I say you sooth, me needeth not to feign;
 So hath your beauty from your heart chased
 Pity, that me availeth not to plain.

Alas! that nature hath in you compassed
So great beauty, that no man may attain
To mercy, though he starve for the pain.
 So hath your beauty from your heart chased
 Pity, that me availeth not to plain;
 For danger holds your mercy in his chain.

III

Escape

Since I from Love escapèd am so fat,
I never think to been in his prison lean;
Since I am free, I count him not a bean.

He may answer, and say this or that;
I do no force, I speak right as I mean.
Since I from Love escapèd am so fat,
I never think to been in his prison lean.

Love hath my name stricken out of his slate,
And he is stricken out of my books clean
Forevermore; there is none other mean.
Since I from Love escapèd am so fat,
I never think to been in his prison lean;
Since I am free, I count him not a bean.

GEOFFREY CHAUCER

TO A LADY

Sweet rose of virtue and of gentleness,
Delightsome lily of every lustiness,
    Richest in bounty and in beauty clear,
    And every virtue that is weenèd dear,
Except only that ye are merciless:

Into your garth this day I did pursue;
There saw I flowers that fresh were of hue,
    Both white and red most lusty were to seen,
    And wholesome herbs upon stalks green;
Yet leaf nor flower find could I none of rue.

I doubt that March with his cold blasts keen
Has slain this gentle herb, that I of mene,
   Whose piteous death does to my heart such pain
   That I would make to plant his root again,
So comforting his leaves unto me been.

WILLIAM DUNBAR

lustiness: delight
weenèd: deemed
garth: garden
that I of mene: that I complain of, or mourn

SONNET XXX

Whether the Turkish new moon minded be
To fill her horns this year on Christian coast;
How Poles' right king means without leave of host
To warm with ill-made fire cold Muscovy;
If French can yet three parts in one agree;
What now the Dutch in their full diets boast;
How Holland hearts, now so good towns be lost,
Trust in the shade of pleasant Orange-tree;
How Ulster likes of that same golden bit
Wherewith my father once made it half tame;
If in the Scotch court be no weltering yet—
These questions busy wits to me do frame.
I, cumbered with good manners, answer do,
But know not how; for still I think of you.

SIR PHILIP SIDNEY

Orange-tree: House of Orange
father: Sir Henry Sidney was President of Wales and
   Lord Deputy of Ireland under Elizabeth
weltering: unrest

CRUELLY, LOVE

cruelly, love
walk the autumn long;
the last flower in whose hair,
thy lips are cold with songs

for which is
first to wither, to pass?
shallowness of sunlight
falls and, cruelly,
across the grass
Comes the
moon

love, walk the
autumn
love, for the last
flower in the hair withers;
thy hair is acold with
dreams,
love thou art frail

—walk the longness of autumn
smile dustily to the people,
for winter
who crookedly care.

E. E. CUMMINGS

GIVE ALL TO LOVE

Give all to love;
Obey thy heart;
Friends, kindred, days,
Estate, good-fame,
Plans, credit and the Muse,—
Nothing refuse.

'Tis a brave master;
Let it have scope:
Follow it utterly,
Hope beyond hope:
High and more high
It dives into noon,
With wing unspent,
Untold intent;
But it is a god,
Knows its own path
And the outlets of the sky.

It was never for the mean;
It requireth courage stout.
Souls above doubt,
Valor unbending,
It will reward,—
They shall return
More than they were,
And ever ascending.

Leave all for love;
Yet, hear me, yet
One word more thy heart behoved,
One pulse more of firm endeavor,—
Keep thee today,
Tomorrow, forever,
Free as an Arab
Of thy beloved.

Cling with life to the maid;
But when the surprise,
First vague shadow of surmise
Flits across her bosom young,
Of a joy apart from thee,
Free be she, fancy-free;
Nor thou detain her vesture's hem,
Nor the palest rose she flung
From her summer diadem.

Though thou loved her as thyself,
As a self of purer clay,
Though her parting dims the day,
Stealing grace from all alive;
Heartily know,
When half-gods go,
The gods arrive.

RALPH WALDO EMERSON

ON HIS MISTRESS

By our first strange and fatal interview,
By all desires which thereof did ensue,
By our long starving hopes, by that remorse
Which my words' masculine persuasive force
Begot in thee, and by the memory
Of hurts, which spies and rivals threaten'd me,
I calmly beg: but by thy father's wrath,
By all pains, which want and divorcement hath,
I conjure thee, and all the oaths which I
And thou have sworn to seal joint constancy,
Here I unswear, and overswear them thus:
Thou shalt not love by ways so dangerous.
Temper, O fair Love, love's impetuous rage;
Be my true Mistress still, not my feign'd page;
I'll go, and, by thy kind leave, leave behind
Thee, only worthy to nurse in my mind,
Thirst to come back—O, if thou die before,
My soul from other lands to thee shall soar.
Thy (else almighty) beauty cannot move
Rage from the seas, nor thy love teach them love,
Nor tame wild Boreas' harshness; thou hast read
How roughly he in pieces shiverèd
Fair Orithea, whom he swore he lov'd.
Fall ill or good, 'tis madness to have prov'd
Dangers unurg'd; feed on this flattery,

154 Come Live with Me

That absent lovers one in th' other be.
Dissemble nothing, not a boy, nor change
Thy body's habit, nor mind's; be not strange
To thyself only: all will spy in thy face
A blushing, womanly, discovering grace.
Richly cloth'd apes, are call'd apes, and as soon
Eclips'd as bright we call the moon the moon.
Men of France, changeable chamelions,
Spittles of diseases, shops of fashions,
Love's fuelers, and the rightest company
Of players, which upon the world's stage be,
Will quickly know thee, and no less, alas!
Th' indifferent Italian, as we pass
His warm land, well content to think thee page,
Will hunt thee with such lust, and hideous rage,
As Lot's fair guests were vex'd. But none of these,
Nor spongy, hydropic Dutch shall thee displease,
If thou stay here. O stay here, for, for thee,
England is only a worthy gallery,
To walk in expectation, till from thence
Our greatest King call thee to his presence.
When I am gone, dream me some happiness,
Nor let thy looks our long hid love confess,
Nor praise, nor dispraise me, nor bless nor curse
Openly love's force, nor in bed fright thy nurse
With midnight startings, crying out, 'Oh, oh
Nurse, O my love is slain, I saw him go
O'er the white Alps alone; I saw him, I,
Assail'd, fight, taken, stabb'd, bleed, fall, and die.'
Augur me better chance, except dread Jove
Think it enough for me to have had thy love.

JOHN DONNE

not my feigned page: she wanted to go with him, disguised
Boreas: north wind, who could not sigh without a gale
Orithea: a nymph beloved by Boreas
Lot's fair guests: two angels (*Genesis, 19*)

WASHINGTON SQUARE

The park-bench strategists have called a truce,
  already the sky is turning violet;
the crowd, that was thick, is thinning away,
  and this is the hour made for you alone.

I do not know who you are, I shall never know:
  a short, immense distance divides us.
        that I like you; I know that you know,
        that Time, ironically, mocks at me . . .

      e air holds its breath
      d the shade under the myrtles becomes blue,
      oke, and am silent, and frozen I look at you:
      vhat does it matter, the things I could tell you?

      nd already the first lamp is lighted;
      another, and another: good-bye, brief nirvana!
The public, well-fed, now resumes
  its chatter round the fountain.

FRANCESCO BIANCO

TO FANNY

I cry your mercy—pity—love,—aye, love!
  Merciful love that tantalizes not,
One-thoughted, never-wandering, guileless love,
  Unmask'd, and being seen—without a blot!
O! let me have thee whole,—all—all—be mine!
  That shape, that fairness, that sweet minor zest
Of love, your kiss,—those hands, those eyes divine,
  That warm, white, lucent, million-pleasured breast,—
Yourself—your soul—in pity give me all,
  Withhold no atom's atom or I die,

Or living on perhaps your wretched thrall,
    Forget, in the mist of idle misery,
Life's purposes,—the palate of my mind
Losing its gust, and my ambition blind!

JOHN KEATS

thrall: slave

THE EXEQUY

Accept, thou shrine of my dead saint,
Instead of dirges this complaint;
And for sweet flowers to crown thy hearse,
Receive a strew of weeping verse
From thy griev'd friend, whom thou might'st see
Quite melted into tears for thee.

    Dear loss! since thy untimely fate
My task hath been to meditate
On thee, on thee: thou art the book,
The library whereon I look
Though almost blind. For thee (lov'd clay)
I languish out not live the day,
Using no other exercise
But what I practise with mine eyes,
By which wet glasses I find out
How lazily time creeps about
To one that mourns—this, only this
My exercise and bus'ness is;
So I compute the weary hours
With sighs dissolvèd into showers.

    Nor wonder if my time go thus
Backward and most preposterous;
Thou hast benighted me, thy set
This eve of blackness did beget,
Who was't my day (though overcast

Before thou had'st thy noon-tide past)
And I remember must in tears
Thou scarce had'st seen so many years
As day tells hours. By thy clear sun
My love and fortune first did run;
But thou wilt never more appear
Folded within my hemisphere,
Since both thy light and motïon
Like a fled star is fall'n and gone,
And 'twixt me and my soul's dear wish
The earth now interposèd is,
Which such a strange eclipse doth make
As ne'er was read in almanack.

    I could allow thee for a time
To darken me and my sad clime,
Were it a month, a year, or ten,
I would thy exile live till then;
And all that space my mirth adjourn,
So thou wouldst promise to return;
And putting off thy ashy shroud
At length disperse this sorrow's cloud.

    But woe is me! the longest date
Too narrow is to calculate
These empty hopes: never shall I
Be so much blest as to descry
A glimpse of thee, till that day come
Which shall the earth to cinders doom,
And a fierce fever must calcine
The body of this world like thine
(My Little World!) That fit of fire
Once off, our bodies shall aspire
To our souls' bliss: then we shall rise,
And view ourselves with clearer eyes
In that calm region where no night
Can hide us from each other's sight.

Meantime, thou hast her, earth: much good
May my harm do thee. Since it stood
With heaven's will I might not call
Her longer mine, I give thee all
My short-liv'd right and interest
In her, whom living I lov'd best;
With a most free and bounteous grief,
I give thee what I could not keep.
Be kind to her, and prithee look
Thou write into thy doomsday book
Each parcel of this rarity
Which in thy casket shrin'd doth lie;
See that thou make thy reck'ning straight,
And yield her back again by weight;
For thou must audit on thy trust
Each grain and atom of this dust,
As thou wilt answer Him that lent,
Not gave thee my dear monument.

So close the ground, and 'bout her shade
Black curtains draw, my bride is laid.

Sleep on, my love, in thy cold bed
Never to be disquieted!
My last good night! Thou wilt not wake
Till I thy fate shall overtake:
Till age, or grief, or sickness must
Marry my body to that dust
It so much loves, and fill the room
My heart keeps empty in thy tomb.
Stay for me there; I will not fail
To meet thee in that hollow vale.
And think not much of my delay;
I am already on the way,
And follow thee with all the speed
Desire can make, or sorrows breed.
Each minute is a short degree,
And ev'ry hour a step towards thee.

At night when I betake to rest,
Next morn I rise nearer my west
Of life, almost by eight hours' sail
Than when sleep breath'd his drowsy gale.

Thus from the sun my bottom steers,
And my day's compass downward bears;
Nor labor I to stem the tide
Through which to thee I swiftly glide.

'Tis true, with shame and grief I yield,
Thou like the van first took'st the field,
And gotten hast the victory
In thus adventuring to die
Before me, whose more years might crave
A just precedence in the grave.
But hark! My pulse like a soft drum
Beats my approach, tells thee I come;
And slow howe'er my marches be,
I shall at last sit down by thee.

The thought of this bids me go on,
And wait my dissolution
With hope and comfort. Dear (forgive
The crime) I am content to live
Divided, with but half a heart,
Till we shall meet and never part.

HENRY KING, BISHOP OF CHICHESTER

Exequy: funeral rite

UPON THE DEATH OF
SIR ALBERT MORTON'S WIFE

He first deceased; she for a little tried
To live without him, liked it not, and died.

SIR HENRY WOTTON

⊰ *NOTES* ⊱

William Walsh was praised by Dryden and Pope, the latter in lines reminiscent of Denham's praise of Cowley (see notes to the first section):

> To him the wit of Greece and Rome was known,
> And every author's merit, but his own.

He possessed a humorous as well as a serious vein; see his "The Despairing Lover" in the following section.

Of Edmund Prestwich, nothing is known except his name and the title of a book and its date, *Hippolitus, Translated out of Seneca: together with divers other Poems,* 1651 (Marshall, *Rare Poems of the Seventeenth Century,* p. 174).

Thomas Hardy started out as an architect. In 1870 he went to North Cornwall with plans for the restoration of St. Juliot church, near fabled, sunken Lyonnesse. When he arrived at the rectory, the door was opened by Emma Lavinia Gifford, the rector's sister-in-law. It was love at first sight. Their marriage was not entirely a happy one; many poems record Hardy's perplexity and grief. When his wife died in 1912, he again wrote love poems about her, and even made a pilgrimage to St. Juliot, at the age of seventy-two. The following poem dates from the earlier period:

DRAWING DETAILS IN AN OLD CHURCH

> I hear the bell-rope sawing,
> And the oil-less axle grind,
> As I sit alone here drawing
> What some Gothic brain designed;
> And I catch the toll that follows
>   From the lagging bell,
> Ere it spreads to hills and hollows
>   Where people dwell.
>
> I ask not whom it tolls for,
> Incurious who he be;
> So, some morrow, when those knolls for
> One unguessed, sound out for me.
> A stranger, loitering under
>   In nave or choir.

May think, too, 'Whose, I wonder?'
But not inquire.

A variation on this theme, by Hardy, appears in the notes to Section 12.

"Love's Harmony" is from *Love's Labour's Lost*, Act IV, Sc. 3.

In modernizing the poems by Chaucer and Dunbar, including "The Complaint of Chaucer to His Purse" in the first section, I have tried to retain their rhythms as well as their sense—as regards the former, not always successfully. The third (and final) line of Chaucer's second rondel is, in the original:

For Daunger halt your mercy in his cheyne.

This "Daunger" has several meanings, as well as variant spellings; the most likely is "disdain," as in this stanza of Dunbar's poem entitled "Of Love Earthly and Divine" (the first line refers to Christ):

I haif a luve farar of face,
Quhome in no denger may haif place,
Quhilk will me guerdon give and grace,
And mercy ay quhen I me mene.

I have a love fairer of face,
In whom no danger may have place,
Who will give me reward and grace,
And mercy whenever I complain.

In "Washington Square," Francesco Bianco expresses the loneliness of his last years: "What does it matter, the things I could tell you?" Little did that young woman know! One who met him termed him "a ravishing conversationalist;" she was tall, and she added: "He could make one forget that he was twice one's age and half one's size."

The theme is found in Yeats and Hardy. I use the draft Yeats sent to Lady Dorothy Wellesley in a letter dated May 24, 1938; a revised version appeared in *Last Poems*, 1939:

POLITICS

'In our time the destiny of man presents
its meaning in political terms.'   THOMAS MANN

Beside that window stands a girl;
I cannot fix my mind
On their analysis of things
That benumb mankind.

> Yet one has travelled and may know
> What he talks about;
> And one's a politician
> That has read and thought.
> Maybe what they say is true
> Of war and war's alarms;
> But O that I were young again
> And held her in my arms.

Hardy's poem is entitled "Faintheart in a Railway Station." He saw, on the platform,

> A radiant stranger, who saw not me.

He hesitated:

> And the wheels moved on. O could it but be
> That I had alighted there!

A similar apparition, or vision, of 1814 stayed in Keats' mind at least four years, which may be a record (see Aileen Ward's *John Keats: The Making of a Poet,* pp. 38–39); he thought it was five when, in 1818, he wrote two sonnets about his experience.

TO A LADY SEEN FOR A FEW MOMENTS AT VAUXHALL

> Time's sea hath been five years at its slow ebb:
>   Long hours have to and fro let creep the sand;
> Since I was tangled in thy beauty's web,
>   And snared by the ungloving of thine hand.
> And yet I never look on midnight sky,
>   But I behold thine eyes' well memory'd light;
> I cannot look upon the rose's dye,
>   But to thy cheek my soul doth take its flight;
> I cannot look on any budding flower,
>   But my fond ear, in fancy at thy lips
> And hearkening for a love-sound, doth devour
>   Its sweets in the wrong sense:—Thou dost eclipse
> Every delight with sweet remembering,
> And grief unto my darling joys dost bring.

The second sonnet was "When I Have Fears That I May Cease to Be," given in Section 1.

By the end of 1818 Keats was engaged to Fanny Brawne. A letter to her in the summer of 1820 provides a vivid background for the sonnet entitled "To Fanny":

My dearest Girl,

    I have been a walk this morning with a book in my hand, but as usual I have been occupied with nothing but you I wish I could say in an agreeable manner. I am tormented day and night. They talk of my going to Italy. 'Tis certain I shall never recover if I am to be so long separate from you yet with all this devotion to you I cannot persuade myself into any confidence of you. Past experience connected with the fact of my long separation from you gives me agonies which are scarcely to be talked of. When your mother comes I shall be very sudden and expert in asking whether you have been to Mrs. Dilke's, for she might say no to make me easy. I am literally worn to death, which seems my only recourse. I cannot forget what has passed. What? nothing with a man of the world, but to me deathful. I will get rid of this as much as possible. When you were in the habit of flirting with Brown you would have left off, could your own heart have felt one half of one pang mine did.

Alas—he was unkind, and unfair; he was also ill. He died in Rome, February 23, 1821.

Bishop King's "Exequy" on the death of his young wife is seldom reprinted in its entirety; but considering its masterly versification, unmatched, in places, by anything in English, the reason may be hard to find. Poe used two of its lines as the epigraph for his story, "The Assignation," and repeated them in the text.

Sir Henry Wotton was an intimate friend of John Donne. He served as ambassador to the Republic of Venice under James I. Mrs. Morton was the widow of a kinsman; Izaak Walton, who wrote Wotton's *Life,* includes a poem by him entitled "Tears Wept at the Grave of Sir Albertus Morton."

8.

Lovers

8. LOVERS

SONG

Go and catch a falling star,
　　Get with child a mandrake root,
Tell me where all past years are,
　　Or who cleft the devil's foot;
Teach me to hear mermaids singing,
Or to keep off envy's stinging,
　　　　And find
　　　　What wind
Serves to advance an honest mind.

If thou be'st born to strange sights,
　　Things invisible to see,
Ride ten thousand days and nights,
　　Till age snow white hairs on thee;
Thou, when thou return'st, wilt tell me
All strange wonders that befell thee,
　　　　And swear
　　　　Nowhere
Lives a woman true and fair.

If thou find'st one, let me know,
　　Such a pilgrimage were sweet;
Yet do not, I would not go
　　Though at next door we might meet;
Though she were true when you met her,
And last till you write your letter,

> Yet she
> Will be
> False, ere I come, to two or three.

JOHN DONNE

AGAINST THEM WHO LAY UNCHASTITY
TO THE SEX OF WOMEN:
A REPLY

> They meet but with unwholesome springs,
>   And summers which infectious are;
> They hear but when the mermaid sings,
>   And only see the falling star,
>   Who ever dare
>   Affirm no woman chaste and fair.

> Go, cure your fevers; and you'll say
>   The dog-days scorch not all the year;
> In copper mines no longer stay,
>   But travel to the west, and there
>   The right ones see,
>   And grant all gold's not alchemy.

> What madman, 'cause the glow-worm's flame
>   Is cold, swears there's no warmth in fire?
> 'Cause some make forfeit of their name,
>   And slave themselves to man's desire,
>   Shall the sex, free
>   From guilt, damn'd to the bondage be?

> Nor grieve, Castara, though t'were frail;
>   Thy virtue then would brighter shine,
> When thy example should prevail,
>   And every woman's faith be thine:
>   And were there none,
>   'Tis majesty to rule alone.

WILLIAM HABINGTON

TO A LADY TO ANSWER DIRECTLY
WITH YEA OR NAY

Madam, withouten many words,
  Once, I am sure, ye will or no:
And if ye will, then leave your bords
  And use your wit and show it so:
And with a beck ye shall me call;
  And if of one, that burneth alway,
Ye have any pity at all,
  Answer him fair with yea, or nay.
If it be yea, I shall be fain;
  If it be nay, friends as before;
Ye shall another man obtain,
  And I mine own and yours no more.

SIR THOMAS WYATT

bords: jests, games

❧ ❦

KIND ARE HER ANSWERS

Kind are her answers,
  But her performance keeps no day;
Breaks time, as dancers
  From their own music when they stray;
  All her free favors and smooth words
Wing my hopes in vain;
O did ever voice so sweet but only feign?
  Can true love yield such delay,
  Converting joy to pain?

Lost is our freedom,
  When we submit to women so;
Why do we need them,

When in their best they work our woe?
There is no wisdom
Can alter ends by fate prefixed;
O why is the good of man with evil mixed?
Never were days yet called two,
But one night went betwixt.

THOMAS CAMPION

A DIALOGUE

'Who is it that this dark night
Underneath my window plaineth?'
It is one who from thy sight
Being (ah) exiled, disdaineth
Every other vulgar light.

'Why, alas, and are you he?
Be not yet those fancies changed?'
Dear, when you find change in me,
Though from me you be estranged,
Let my change to ruin be.

'Well, in absence this will die;
Leave to see, and leave to wonder.'
Absence sure will help, if I
Can learn how myself to sunder
From what in my heart doth lie.

'But time will these thoughts remove;
Time doth work what no man knoweth.'
Time doth as the subject prove;
With time still the affection groweth
In the faithful turtle dove.

'What if you new beauties see;
Will not they stir new affection?'

I will think they pictures be,
Image-like of saints' perfection,
Poorly counterfeiting thee.

'But your reason's purest light
Bids you leave such minds to nourish.'
Dear, do reason no such spite;
Never doth thy beauty flourish
More than in my reason's sight.

'But the wrongs love bears will make
Love at length leave undertaking.'
No, the more fools it do shake,
In a ground of so firm making,
Deeper still they drive the stake.

'Peace, I think that some give ear;
Come no more lest I get anger.'
Bliss, I will my bliss forbear,
Fearing, sweet, you to endanger;
But my soul shall harbor there.

'Well, begone, begone I say,
Lest that Argus' eyes perceive you.'
O unjust is Fortune's sway,
Which can make me thus to leave you,
And from louts to run away.

SIR PHILIP SIDNEY

Argus: the hundred-eyed; here, watchful guard-
ians

WESTERN WIND, WHEN WILT THOU BLOW

Western wind, when wilt thou blow,
The small rain down can rain?
Christ, if my love were in my arms,
And I in my bed again!

ANON.

HORACE, BOOK I, ODE 5

What slender youth bedewed with liquid odors
Courts thee on roses in some pleasant cave,
   Pyrrha? For whom bind'st thou
   In wreaths thy golden hair,
Plain in thy neatness? O how oft shall he
On faith and changed gods complain, and seas
   Rough with black winds, and storms
   Unwonted shall admire,
Who now enjoys three credulous, all gold,
Who always vacant, always amiable,
   Hopes thee; of flattering gales
   Unmindful. Hapless they
To whom thou, untried, seem'st fair. Me in my vowed
Picture the sacred wall declares t'have hung
   My dank and dropping weeds
   To the stern god of sea.

JOHN MILTON

PASTORAL VERSES ON TWO LOVERS

Down lay the shepherd swain,
   so sober and demure,
Wishing for his wench again,
   so bonny and so pure;
With his head on hillock low,
   and his arms akimbo,
And all was for the loss of his
   hey nonny nonny no.

His tears fell as thin
   as water from the still,
His hair upon his chin
   grew like thyme upon a hill,

His cherry cheeks pale as snow
   did testify his mickle woe,
And all was for the loss of his
   hey nonny nonny no.

Sweet she was, as kind a love
   as ever fettered swain;
Never such a dainty one
   shall man enjoy again.
Set a thousand in a row,
   I forbid that any show
Ever the like of her
   hey nonny nonny no.

Face she had of filbert hue,
   and bosomed like the swan;
Back she had of bended ewe,
   and waisted by a span;
Hair she had as black as crow,
   from the head unto the toe,
Down, down all over her
   hey nonny nonny no.

With her mantle tucked up high
   she fodderèd her flock;
So buxom and alluringly
   her knee upheld her smock;
So nimbly did she use to go,
   so smooth she danced on tip-toe,
That all the men were fond of her
   hey nonny nonny no.

She smilèd like a holiday,
   she simpered like the spring,
She pranked it like a popinjay,
   and like a swallow [did] sing;
She tripped it like a barren doe,
   she strutted like a gor-crow,

Which made the men so fond of her
hey nonny nonny no.

To sport it on the merry down,
to dance the lively hay;
To wrestle for a green gown
in heat of all the day,
Never would she say me no,
yet methought I had, though,
Never enough of her
hey nonny nonny no.

But gone she is, the prettiest lass
that ever trod on plain;
Whatever hath betide of her,
blame not the shepherd swain;
For why? she was her own foe,
and gave herself the overthrow,
By being so frank of her
hey nonny nonny no.

ANON.

mickle: great
filbert hue: color of hazel nut
pranked: showed off
popinjay: parrot on pole as mark to
shoot at, here "conceited"
gor-crow: carrion crow
lively hay: a country dance
green gown: roll in the grass
betide: become

TIME IS A FEATHERED THING

Time is a feathered thing
And, whilst I praise
The sparklings of thy looks and call them rays,
Takes wing,
Leaving behind him as he flies
An unperceivèd dimness in thine eyes.

His minutes, whilst they're told,
    Do make us old;
And every sand of his fleet glass,
Increasing age as it doth pass,
Insensibly sows wrinkles there
Where flowers and roses do appear.
Whilst we do speak, our fire
Doth into ice expire,
    Flames turn to frost;
    And ere we can
Know how our crow turns swan,
Or how a silver snow
Springs there where jet did grow,
Our fading spring is in dull winter lost.

Since, then, the night hath hurled
    Darkness, love's shade,
Over its enemy, the day, and made
      The world
Just such a blind and shapeless thing
As 'twas before light did from darkness spring,
    Let us employ its treasure
    And make shade pleasure:
Let's number out the hours by blisses,
And count the minutes by our kisses;
    Let the heavens new motions feel
    And by our embraces wheel;
    And whilst we try the way
    By which love doth convey
      Soul unto soul,
      And mingling so
Makes them such raptures know
As makes them entrancèd lie
    In mutual ecstasy,
Let the harmonious spheres in music roll!

JASPER MAYNE

TO HIS COY MISTRESS

Had we but world enough, and time,
This coyness, lady, were no crime.
We would sit down, and think which way
To walk, and pass our long love's day.
Thou by the Indian Ganges' side
Should'st rubies find; I by the tide
Of Humber would complain. I would
Love you ten years before the Flood,
And you should if you please refuse
Till the conversion of the Jews.
My vegetable love should grow
Vaster than empires, and more slow:
An hundred years should go to praise
Thine eyes, and on thy forehead gaze;
Two hundred to adore each breast,
But thirty thousand to the rest;
An age at least to every part,
And the last age should show your heart,
For, lady, you deserve this state,
Nor would I love at lower rate.
   But at my back I always hear
Time's wingèd chariot hurrying near;
And yonder all before us lie
Deserts of vast eternity.
Thy beauty shall no more be found,
Nor, in thy marble vault, shall sound
My echoing song—then worms shall try
That long preserv'd virginity,
And your quaint honor turn to dust,
And into ashes all my lust:
The grave's a fine and private place,
But none I think do there embrace.
   Now therefore, while the youthful hue
Sits on thy skin like morning dew,
And while thy willing soul transpires

At every pore with instant fires,
Now let us sport us while we may;
And now, like am'rous birds of prey,
Rather at once our time devour,
Than languish in his slow-chapped power.
Let us roll all our strength, and all
Our sweetness, up into one ball,
And tear our pleasures with rough strife,
Thorough the iron gates of life.
Thus, though we cannot make our sun
Stand still, yet we will make him run.

ANDREW MARVELL

slow-chapped: *i.e.,* of jaws

THE KISS

Hold not your lips so close—dispense
Treasures, perfumes and life from thence;
Squeeze not those full-ripe cherries, this
Becomes a simper, not a kiss.
There's danger to lock up your breath,
It cousin-germane is to death;
None bags up wind, the merchant swears,
Unless some wrinkled Laplanders.
What needs this guard? It is small sense
Thus to hedge in a double fence;
Closed lips express but silent blisses,
And at the best are but dumb kisses.
You are with Cupid little kind
To make him dumb as well as blind;
Such smacks but show a silent state—

Kisses should be articulate.
An open-mouthed kiss speaks sense,
It is the lover's eloquence;
Let yours speak out then! there's no bliss
To the pronunciation of a kiss.

THOMAS SHIPMAN

AN ELEGY

Since you must go, and I must bid farewell,
  Hear, Mistress, your departing servant tell
What it is like, and do not think they can
  Be idle words, though of a parting man.
It is as if a night should shade noonday,
  Or that the sun was here, but forc'd away,
And we were left under that hemisphere
  Where we must feel it dark for half a year.
What fate is this, to change men's days and hours,
  To shift their seasons, and destroy their powers!
Alas, I have lost my heat, my blood, my prime—
  Winter is come a quarter ere his time,
My health will leave me; and when you depart,
  How shall I do, sweet Mistress, for my heart?
You would restore it? No, that's worth a fear,
  As if it were not worthy to be there;
Oh, keep it still, for it had rather be
  Your sacrifice than here remain with me,
And so I spare it. Come what can become
  Of me, I'll softly tread unto my tomb,
Or like a ghost walk silent amongst men,
  Till I may see both it and you again.

BEN JONSON

SONG

Phyllis is my only joy,
  Faithless as the winds or seas,
Sometimes cunning, sometimes coy,
  Yet she never fails to please;
    If with a frown
    I am cast down,
    Phyllis smiling
    And beguiling
Makes me happier than before.

Though alas! too late I find
  Nothing can her fancy fix,
Yet the moment she is kind
  I forgive her with her tricks;
    Which though I see,
    I can't get free—
    She deceiving,
    I believing—
What need lovers wish for more?

SIR CHARLES SEDLEY

LOVE AND LIFE: A SONG

All my past life is mine no more,
  The flying hours are gone,
Like transitory dreams given o'er,
Whose images are kept in store
  By memory alone.

The time that is to come is not,
  How can it then be mine?
The present moment's all my lot,
And that, as fast as it is got,
  Phyllis, is wholly thine.

Then talk not of inconstancy,
　　False hearts and broken vows;
If I by miracle can be
This live-long minute true to thee,
　　'Tis all that heaven allows.

JOHN WILMOT, EARL OF ROCHESTER

ॐ ॐ

DUET

LORENZO

The moon shines bright: in such a night as this,
When the sweet wind did gently kiss the trees
And they did make no noise, in such a night
Troilus methinks mounted the Troyan walls,
And sigh'd his soul toward the Grecian tents,
Where Cressid lay that night.

JESSICA

In such a night

Did Thisbe fearfully o'ertrip the dew,
And saw the lion's shadow ere himself,
And ran dismay'd away.

LORENZO

In such a night

Stood Dido with a willow in her hand
Upon the wild sea-banks, and waft her love
To come again to Carthage.

JESSICA

In such a night

Medea gather'd the enchanted herbs
That did renew old Æson.

LORENZO

In such a night

Did Jessica steal from the wealthy Jew,
And with an unthrift love did run from Venice,
As far as Belmont.

JESSICA

In such a night

Did young Lorenzo swear he lov'd her well,
Stealing her soul with many vows of faith,
And ne'er a true one.

LORENZO

In such a night

Did pretty Jessica, like a little shrew,
Slander her love, and he forgave it her.

JESSICA

I would out-night you, did nobody come.
[STEPHANO *comes, and goes*]

LORENZO

How sweet the moonlight sleeps upon this bank!
Here will we sit, and let the sounds of music
Creep in our ears: soft stillness and the night
Become the touches of sweet harmony.
Sit, Jessica: look, how the floor of heaven
Is thick inlaid with patines of bright gold;
There's not the smallest orb which thou behold'st
But in his motion like an angel sings,
Still quiring to the young-eyed cherubins.
Such harmony is in immortal souls,
But, whilst this muddy vesture of decay
Doth grossly close it in, we cannot hear it.
[*Enter* MUSICIANS]
Come, ho! and wake Diana with a dream:

With sweetest touches pierce your mistress' ear,
And draw her home with music.

JESSICA

I am never merry when I hear sweet music.

LORENZO

The reason is, your spirits are attentive:
For do but note a wild and wanton herd,
Or race of youthful and unhandled colts,
Fetching mad bounds, bellowing and neighing loud,
Which is the hot condition of their blood—
If they but hear perchance a trumpet sound,
Or any air of music touch their ears,
You shall perceive them make a mutual stand,
Their savage eyes turn'd to a modest gaze
By the sweet power of music: therefore the poet
Did feign that Orpheus drew trees, stones, and floods;
Since nought so stockish, hard, and full of rage,
But music for the time doth change his nature.
The man that hath no music in himself,
Nor is not mov'd with concord of sweet sounds,
Is fit for treasons, stratagems, and spoils;
The motions of his spirit are dull as night,
And his affections dark as Erebus:
Let no such man be trusted. Mark the music.

WILLIAM SHAKESPEARE

willow: symbol of deserted lover—hence, "to wear the willow," mourn for one's beloved
Æson: father of Jason of the Golden Fleece
wealthy Jew: Shylock, Jessica's father in *The Merchant of Venice*
Belmont: near Portia's house (scene of the "Duet")
Diana: goddess of the moon, in love with a mortal shepherd; hence Portia's observation: "Peace, ho! the moon sleeps with Endymion," while the music is playing
Erebus: Hades

OVID, BOOK I, ELEGY 5

In summer's heat and mid-time of the day,
To rest my limbs upon a bed I lay;
One window shut, the other open stood,
Which gave such light as twinkles in a wood
Like twilight gleams at setting of the sun,
Or night being past and yet not day begun;
Such light to shamefast maidens must be shown,
Where they may sport and seem to be unknown.
Then came Corinna in a long loose gown,
Her white neck hid with tresses hanging down,
Resembling fair Semiramis going to bed,
Or Lais of a thousand wooers sped.
I snatched her gown—being thin, the harm was small,
Yet strove she to be covered therewithal,
And striving thus, as one that would be cast,
Betrayed herself and yielded at the last.
Stark naked as she stood before mine eye,
Not one wen in her body could I spy.
What arms and shoulders did I touch and see!
How apt her breasts were to be pressed by me!
How smooth a belly under her waist saw I,
How large a leg, and what a lusty thigh!
To leave the rest, all liked me passing well;
I clinged her naked body, down she fell;
Judge you the rest. Being tired, she bade me kiss—
Jove send me more such afternoons as this.

CHRISTOPHER MARLOWE

Semiramis: a Babylonian queen
Lais: a Roman courtesan

THE WAKENING

On a time the amorous Silvy
Said to her shepherd, 'Sweet, how do ye?
Kiss me this once and then God be wi' ye,
          My sweetest dear!
Kiss me this once and then God be wi' ye,
For now the morning draweth near.'

With that, her fairest bosom showing,
Op'ning her lips, rich perfumes blowing,
She said, 'Now kiss me and be going,
          My sweetest dear!
Kiss me this once and then be going,
For now the morning draweth near.'

With that the shepherd waked from sleeping,
And spying where the day was peeping,
He said, 'Now take my soul in keeping,
          My sweetest dear!
Kiss me and take my soul in keeping,
Since I must go, now day is near.'

                        ANON.

SONG

For her gait, if she be walking;
Be she sitting, I desire her
For her state's sake; and admire her
For her wit if she be talking;
    Gait and state and wit approve her;
    For which all and each I love her.

Be she sullen, I commend her
For a modest. Be she merry,
For a kind one her prefer I.
Briefly, everything doth lend her
  So much grace, and so approve her,
  That for everything I love her.

WILLIAM BROWNE OF TAVISTOCK

THE AUTHOR'S RESOLUTION IN A SONNET

Shall I, wasting in despair,
Die because a woman's fair?
Or make pale my cheeks with care
'Cause another's rosy are?
  Be she fairer than the day,
  Or the flowery meads in May,
  If she think not well of me,
  What care I how fair she be?

Shall my silly heart be pined
'Cause I see a woman kind?
Or a well disposèd nature
Joinèd with a lovely feature?
  Be she meeker, kinder than
  Turtle-dove or pelican,
  If she be not so to me,
  What care I how kind she be?

Shall a woman's virtues move
Me to perish for her love?
Or her well deservings known
Make me quite forget mine own?
  Be she with that goodness blest
  Which may merit name of best,
  If she be not such to me,
  What care I how good she be?

'Cause her fortune seems too high,
Shall I play the fool and die?
She that bears a noble mind,
If not outward helps she find,
  Thinks that with them he would do,
  That without them dares her woo,
  And unless that mind I see,
  What care I how great she be?

Great, or good, or kind, or fair,
I will ne'er the more despair:
If she love me (this believe)
I will die ere she shall grieve.
  If she slight me when I woo,
  I can scorn and let her go,
  For if she be not for me,
  What care I for whom she be?

GEORGE WITHER

Sonnet: in old sense, "song"
Turtle-dove: noted for soft cooing and affection for mate
pelican: in fable, feeding its young with
  own blood
fortune: station

ঌ ঌ

THE CONSTANT LOVER

Out upon it, I have loved
  Three whole days together!
And am like to love three more,
  If it prove fair weather.

Time shall moult away his wings
    Ere he shall discover
In the whole wide world again
    Such a constant lover.

But the spite on't is, no praise
    Is due at all to me:
Love with me had made no stays,
    Had it any been but she.

Had it any been but she,
    And that very face,
There had been at least ere this
    A dozen dozen in her place.

SIR JOHN SUCKLING

THE DESPAIRING LOVER

Distracted with care
For Phyllis the fair,
Since nothing could move her,
Poor Damon, her lover,
Resolves in despair
    No longer to languish,
    Nor bear so much anguish,
But, mad with his love,
    To a precipice goes,
Where a leap from above
    Would finish his woes.

When in rage he came there,
    Beholding how steep
The sides did appear,
    And the bottom how deep,

His torments projecting,
And sadly reflecting
That a lover forsaken
    A new love may get,
But a neck when once broken
    Can never be set,
And, that he could die
    Whenever he would,
Whereas he could live
    But as long as he could,
How grievous soever
    The torment might grow,
He scorned to endeavor
    To finish it so,
But, bold, unconcerned
    At thoughts of the pain,
He calmly returned
    To his cottage again.

WILLIAM WALSH

❧ ❦

UPON HIS MISTRESS DANCING

I stood and saw my mistress dance,
    Silent, and with so fixed an eye,
Some might suppose me in a trance;
    But being askèd, why?
By one that knew I was in love,
    I could not but impart
My wonder, to behold her move
    So nimbly with a marble heart.

JAMES SHIRLEY

THE DOUBLE ROCK

Since thou hast viewed some Gorgon, and art grown
  A solid stone,
To bring again to softness thy hard heart
  Is past my art.
Ice may relent to water in a thaw;
But stone made flesh Love's chemistry ne'er saw.

Therefore, by thinking on thy hardness, I
  Will petrify;
And so within our double quarry's womb,
  Dig our love's tomb.

Thus strangely will our difference agree,
And, with ourselves, amaze the world, to see
How both revenge and sympathy consent
To make two rocks each other's monument.

HENRY KING, BISHOP OF CHICHESTER

TO ROSES IN THE BOSOM OF CASTARA

Ye blushing virgins happy are
In the chaste nunnery of her breasts,
For he'd profane so chaste a fair,
Whoe'er should call them Cupid's nests.

Transplanted thus how bright ye grow,
How rich a perfume do ye yield?
In some close garden cowslips so
Are sweeter than i' th' open field.

In those white cloisters live secure
From the rude blasts of wanton breath,
Each hour more innocent and pure,
Till you shall wither into death.

Then that which living gave you room
Your glorious sepulcher shall be:
There wants no marble for a tomb
Whose breast has marble been to me.

WILLIAM HABINGTON

fair: *i.e.*, the lady

TO ETHELINDA

*On Her Doing My Verses the Honor of Wearing Them
in Her Bosom.—Written at Thirteen*

Happy verses! that were prest
In fair Ethelinda's breast!
Happy Muse, that didst embrace
The sweet, the heav'nly-fragrant place!
Tell me, is the omen true,
Shall the bard arrive there too?

Oft through my eyes my soul has flown,
And wanton'd on that ivory throne:
There with ecstatic transport burn'd,
And thought it was to heav'n return'd.
Tell me, is the omen true,
Shall the body follow too?

When first at nature's early birth,
Heav'n sent a man upon the earth,
Ev'n Eden was more fruitful found,
When Adam came to till the ground:
Shall then those breasts be fair in vain,
And only rise to fall again?

No, no, fair nymph—for no such end
Did heav'n to thee its bounty lend;
That breast was ne'er design'd by fate,
For verse, or things inanimate;
Then throw them from that downy bed,
And take the poet in their stead.

CHRISTOPHER SMART

TO LUCASTA, GOING TO THE WARS

Tell me not, Sweet, I am unkind,
    That from the nunnery
Of thy chaste breast and quiet mind
    To war and arms I fly.

True, a new mistress now I chase,
    The first foe in the field;
And with a stronger faith embrace
    A sword, a horse, a shield.

Yet this inconstancy is such
    As thou too shalt adore;
I could not love thee, Dear, so much,
    Loved I not Honour more.

RICHARD LOVELACE

THE BRIDEGROOM

Call me not false, beloved,
    If, from thy scarce-known breast
So little time removed,
    In other arms I rest.

For this more ancient bride,
  Whom coldly I embrace,
Was constant at my side
  Before I saw thy face.

Our marriage, often set—
  By miracle delayed—
At last is consummate,
  And cannot be unmade.

Live, then, whom life shall cure,
  Almost, of memory,
And leave us to endure
  Its immortality.

RUDYARD KIPLING

CYNARA!

Non sum qualis eram bonae sub regno Cynara

Last night, ah, yesternight, betwixt her lips and mine
There fell thy shadow, Cynara! thy breath was shed
Upon my soul between the kisses and the wine;
And I was desolate and sick of an old passion,
  Yea, I was desolate and bow'd my head:
I have been faithful to thee, Cynara! in my fashion.

All night upon mine heart I felt her warm heart beat,
Night-long within mine arms in love and sleep she lay;
Surely the kisses of her bought red mouth were sweet;
But I was desolate and sick of an old passion,
  When I awoke and found the dawn was gray:
I have been faithful to thee, Cynara! in my fashion.

I have forgot much, Cynara! gone with the wind,
Flung roses, roses, riotously with the throng,
Dancing, to put thy pale lost lilies out of mind;

But I was desolate and sick of an old passion,
   Yea, all the time, because the dance was long:
I have been faithful to thee, Cynara! in my fashion.

I cried for madder music and for stronger wine,
But when the feast is finish'd and the lamps expire,
Then falls thy shadow, Cynara! the night is thine;
And I am desolate and sick of an old passion,
   Yea, hungry for the lips of my desire:
I have been faithful to thee, Cynara! in my fashion.

ERNEST DOWSON

THE TELEPHONE

'When I was just as far as I could walk
From here today,
There was an hour
All still
When leaning with my head against a flower
I heard you talk.
Don't say I didn't, for I heard you say—
You spoke from that flower on the window sill—
Do you remember what it was you said?'

'First tell me what it was you thought you heard.'

'Having found the flower and driven a bee away,
I leaned my head,
And holding by the stalk,
I listened and I thought I caught the word—
What was it? Did you call me by my name?
Or did you say—
Someone said "Come"—I heard it as I bowed.'

'I may have thought as much, but not aloud.'

'Well, so I came.'

ROBERT FROST

A WOMAN HOMER SUNG

If any man drew near
When I was young,
I thought, 'He holds her dear,'
And shook with hate and fear.
But O! 'twas bitter wrong
If he could pass her by
With an indifferent eye.

Whereon I wrote and wrought,
And now, being grey,
I dream that I have brought
To such a pitch my thought
That coming time can say,
'He shadowed in a glass
What thing her body was.'

For she had fiery blood
When I was young,
And trod so sweetly proud
As 'twere upon a cloud,
A woman Homer sung,
That life and letters seem
But an heroic dream.

WILLIAM BUTLER YEATS

⚒ *NOTES* ⚒

William Habington's reply to Donne's famous lyric was no surprise to his contemporaries, who knew him to be devoted to one woman, the daughter of William, Lord Powis, whom he has celebrated under the name of Castara; her real name was Lucy. He wooed her, married her, and continued to write in her praise in their home in Hindlip, Worcestershire.

Milton's translation from Horace was accompanied by this note: "Rendered almost word for word without rhyme, according to the Latin measure, as near as the language will permit."

The lady in "Pastoral Verses on Two Lovers" was the wife of John Overall, Dean of St. Paul's, afterwards Bishop of Coventry and Lich-field, 1614, and of Norwich, 1618, in which year he died. He was, says John Aubrey, "most remarkable by his wife, who was the greatest beauty of her time in England," adding: "She was not more beautiful than she was obliging and kind, and was so tender-hearted that (truly) she could scarce deny anyone." One of her admirers was Sir John Selby, of Yorkshire, the "shepherd swain" of the poem. A popular song about the lovers had the following stanza, also quoted by Aubrey:

> The Dean of St. Paul's did search for his wife,
>   and where d' ee think he found her?
> Even upon Sir John Selby's bed,
>   as flat as any flounder.

(From *Aubrey's Brief Lives,* edited by Oliver Lawson Dick.)

Jasper Mayne's "Time is a Feathered Thing" is from *The Amorous War,* a tragi-comedy, 1648. In addition to another play, *The City Match,* which Pepys saw in 1668 and termed "silly," Mayne wrote a number of poems in Latin and English. A clergyman, and a royalist, his fortunes suffered in the civil war; but with the Restoration he was reinstated in his benefices, appointed a canon of Christ Church, Oxford, archdeacon of Chichester, and chaplain-in-ordinary to Charles II. It is perhaps unnecessary to call attention to the resemblances between Mayne's poem and the better known "To His Coy Mistress" by Marvell.

As Ranger and Keeper of Woodstock Park, the young Earl of Rochester was able to entertain his friends, the rakes and wits of Whitehall, in the High Lodge, with its spectacular view to the distant Cotswolds. Most of them wrote verse, and the resemblances in their poems are often due to the subjects they chose while sojourning there. Sir George Etherege, who wrote a play about Rochester, is also the author of a poem which resembles "Love and Life: A Song." It is called "To a Lady Asking Him How Long He Would Love Her":

> It is not, Celia, in our power
>   To say how long our love will last;
> It may be we within this hour
>   May lose those joys we now do taste;
> The blessèd, that immortal be,
> From change in love are only free.
>
> Then since we mortal lovers are,
>   Ask not how long our love will last;
> But while it does, let us take care
>   Each minute be with pleasure past:
> Were it not madness to deny
> To live because we're sure to die?

There is in it, as well, an echo from Catullus (see Jonson's poem, Section 5, addressed to another Celia).

Thomas Shipman was a Northamptonshire squire and royalist. His *Carolina, or Loyal Poems* appeared posthumously, 1683 (Marshall, *Rare Poems of the Seventeenth Century,* p. 187).

"The Wakening" is from John Attye's *First Book of Airs,* 1622.

Ernest Dowson's "Cynara!" gets its motto from an ode by Horace (IV, 1) the opening of which, in Ben Jonson's translation, is as follows:

> Venus, again thou mov'st a war
> Long intermitted; pray thee, pray thee, **spare!**
>   I am not such, as in the reign
>   Of the good Cynara I was. . . .

9.

Ladies

9. LADIES

HERE SHE WAS WONT TO GO!
AND HERE! AND HERE!

Here she was wont to go! and here! and here!
Just where those daisies, pinks and violets grow:
The world may find the Spring by following her,
For other print her airy steps ne'er left.
Her treading would not bend a blade of grass!
Or shake the downy blowball from his stalk!
But like the soft west wind, she shot along,
And where she went, the flowers took thickest root,
As she had sow'd them with her odorous foot.

BEN JONSON

UPON JULIA'S CLOTHES

Whenas in silks my Julia goes,
Then, then (methinks) how sweetly flows
That liquefaction of her clothes.

Next, when I cast mine eyes and see
That brave vibration each way free—
O how that glittering taketh me!

ROBERT HERRICK

199

MADRIGAL

My Love in her attire doth show her wit,
   It doth so well become her;
For every season she hath dressings fit,
   For winter, spring, and summer.
      No beauty she doth miss
      When all her robes are on;
      But Beauty's self she is
      When all her robes are gone.

                ANON.

MY SILKS AND FINE ARRAY

My silks and fine array,
   My smiles and languished air,
By love are driven away;
   And mournful lean Despair
Brings me yew to deck my grave:
Such end true lovers have.

His face is fair as heaven
   When springing buds unfold;
O, why to him was 't given,
   Whose heart is wintry cold?
His breast is love's all-worshipped tomb,
Where all love's pilgrims come.

Bring me an axe and spade,
   Bring me a winding-sheet;
When I my grave have made,
   Let winds and tempests beat:
Then down I'll lie, as cold as clay.
True love doth pass away!

              WILLIAM BLAKE

GIVE BEAUTY ALL HER RIGHT

Give beauty all her right,
She's not to one form tied;
Each shape yields fair delight,
Where her perfections bide.
Helen, I grant, might pleasing be,
And Ros'mond was as sweet as she.

Some the quick eye commends;
Some swelling lips and red;
Pale looks have many friends,
Through sacred sweetness bred.
Meadows have flowers that pleasure move,
Though roses are the flowers of love.

Free beauty is not bound
To one unmovèd clime;
She visits every ground,
And favors every time.
Let the old loves with mine compare,
My sovereign is as sweet and fair.

THOMAS CAMPION

Ros'mond: Henry II's mistress

❧ ❦

POLITE SONG

*"A person of genius has to do something;
Sarah Bernhardt slept in her coffin."—W. B. Yeats*

Prester John had apes of gold
To talk away the almond hours;
King Alexander, we are told,
Had sudden birds in golden flowers

To bubble out music all day long,
And ravish his dark heart with song.

While you, who've yet no coffin made
(Thank God!) to put your beauty in,
Choose other ways to fool the shade
That haunts the genius of your skin,
And come—O grace unmerited!—
To ravish darkness in this bed.

THEODORE SPENCER

THE MASK

'Put off that mask of burning gold
With emerald eyes.'
'O no, my dear, you make so bold
To find if hearts be wild and wise,
And yet not cold.'

'I would but find what's there to find,
Love or deceit.'
'It was the mask engaged your mind,
And after set your heart to beat,
Not what's behind.'

'But lest you are my enemy,
I must enquire.'
'O no, my dear, let all that be;
What matter, so there is but fire
In you, in me?'

WILLIAM BUTLER YEATS

ANOTHER DARK LADY

Think not, because I wonder where you fled,
That I would lift a pin to see you there;
You may, for me, be prowling anywhere,
So long as you show not your little head:
No dark and evil story of the dead
Would leave you less pernicious or less fair—
Not even Lilith, with her famous hair;
And Lilith was the devil, I have read.

I cannot hate you, for I loved you then.
The woods were golden then. There was a road
Through beeches; and I said their smooth feet showed
Like yours. Truth must have heard me from afar,
For I shall never have to learn again
That yours are cloven as no beech's are.

EDWIN ARLINGTON ROBINSON

CATHERINE TAKES A STROLL

She hurries. . . .
Her life is one long Marathon.
She tarries. . . .
Only to put something pretty on.

Never still,
She hastens this way, then that,
Up steep hill:
To get to top as quick as scat.

Once there,
She'll not think it time to stop.
Sans care
She'll scamper down, then—what else but up?

Another mile!
The angels must love to see her run,
They smile:
To see her speeding is such fun!

The wind stirs:
She creates breezes when she walks.
The wind purrs:
Grows gentle when she stops and talks.

JOHN COURNOS

THE GHOST

'Who knocks?' 'I, who was beautiful,
   Beyond all dreams to restore,
I, from the roots of the dark thorn am hither,
   And knock on the door.'

'Who speaks?' 'I—once was my speech
   Sweet as the bird's on the air,
When echo lurks by the waters to heed;
   'Tis I speak thee fair.'

'Dark is the hour!' 'Ay, and cold.'
   'Lone is my house.' 'Ah, but mine?'
'Sight, touch, lips, eyes yearned in vain.'
   'Long dead these to thine. . . .'

Silence. Still faint on the porch
   Brake the flames of the stars.
In gloom groped a hope-wearied hand
   Over keys, bolts, and bars.

A face peered. All the grey night
   In chaos of vacancy shone;
Nought but vast sorrow was there—
   The sweet cheat gone.

WALTER DE LA MARE

THE LOOKING-GLASS

So well I love thee, as without thee I
Love nothing. If I might choose, I'd rather die
Than be one day debarred thy company.

Since beasts and plants do grow, and live and move,
Beasts are those men that such a life approve;
He only lives that deadly is in love.

The corn that in the ground is sown first dies,
And of one seed do many ears arise;
Love, this world's corn, by dying multiplies.

The seeds of love first by thy eyes were thrown
Into a ground untill'd, a heart unknown
To bear such fruit, till by thy hands 'twas sown.

Look: as your looking-glass by chance may fall,
Divide, and break in many pieces small,
And yet shows forth the selfsame face in all—

Proportions, features, graces just the same,
And in the smallest piece as well the name
Of fairest one deserves as in the richest frame—

So all my thoughts are pieces but of you,
Which, put together, makes a glass so true,
As I therein no other's face but yours can view.

MICHAEL DRAYTON

TO ONE ADMIRING HERSELF IN A LOOKING-GLASS

Fair lady, when you see the grace
Of beauty in your looking-glass—
A stately forehead smooth and high
And full of princely majesty;

A sparkling eye, no gem so fair,
Whose lustre dims the Cyprian star;
A glorious cheek divinely sweet
Wherein both roses kindly meet;
A cherry lip that would entice
Even gods to kiss at any price—
You think no beauty is so rare
That with your shadow might compare,
That your reflection is alone
The thing that men most dote upon.
Madam, alas, your glass doth lie,
And you are much deceived, for I
A beauty know of richer grace;
Sweet, be not angry—'tis your face.
Hence then, oh learn more mild to be,
And leave to lay your blame on me,
If me your rëal substance move
When you so much your shadow love.
Wise nature would not let your eye
Look on her own bright majesty,
Which had you once but gazed upon,
You could—except yourself—love none.
What then you cannot love, let me,
That face I can, you cannot, see.
Now you have what to love, you'll say
'What then is left for me, I pray?'
My face, sweetheart, if it please thee:
That which you can, I cannot, see;
So either love shall gain his due—
Yours, sweet in me, and mine in you.

THOMAS RANDOLPH

Cyprian: pertaining to Cyprus, reputed birth-
place of Aphrodite

THE LADY WHO OFFERS HER
LOOKING-GLASS TO VENUS

Venus, take my votive glass:
Since I am not what I was,
What from this day I shall be,
Venus, let me never see.

MATTHEW PRIOR

IN PRAISE OF HIS LOVE

Give place, ye lovers, here before
That spent your boasts and brags in vain;
My lady's beauty passeth more
The best of yours, I dare well sayen,
Than doth the sun the candle light
Or brightest day the darkest night.

And thereto hath a troth as just
As had Penelope the fair;
For what she saith, ye may it trust,
As it by writing sealèd were;
And virtues hath she many moe
Than I with pen have skill to show.

I could rehearse, if that I would,
The whole effect of Nature's plaint,
When she had lost the perfect mould,
The like to whom she could not paint;
With wringing hands how she did cry,
And what she said, I know it, I.

I know she swore with raging mind,
Her kingdom only set apart,
There was no loss by law of kind

That could have gone so near her heart;
And this was chiefly all her pain:
'She could not make the like again.'

Sith Nature thus gave her the praise,
To be the chiefest work she wrought,
In faith, methinks, some better ways
On your behalf might well be sought
Than to compare, as ye have done,
To match the candle with the sun.

HENRY HOWARD, EARL OF SURREY

troth: pledged word; here, Penelope's faith-
 fulness
law of kind: nature in general

HER PERFECTIONS

What tongue can her perfections tell,
In whose each part all pens may dwell—
Her hair fine threads of finest gold,
In curlèd knots man's thought to hold—
But that her forehead says, 'In me,
A whiter beauty you may see.'
Whiter indeed, more white than snow
Which on cold winter's face doth grow,
That doth present those even brows
Whose equal line their angles bows,
Like to the moon when, after change,
Her hornèd head abroad doth range,
And arches be two heavenly lids
Whose wink each bold attempt forbids.
For the black stars those spheres contain,
The matchless pair even praise doth stain;
No lamp whose light by art is got,
No sun which shines and seeth not,
Can liken them, without all peer,

Save one as much as other clear,
Which only thus unhappy be
Because themselves they cannot see.
Her cheeks with kindly claret spread,
Aurora-like, new out of bed,
Or like the fresh queen-apple's side,
Blushing at sight of Phoebus' pride.
Her nose, her chin, pure ivory wears
No purer than the pretty ears,
But that therein appears some blood
Like wine and milk that mingled stood,
In whose incirclets if ye gaze
Your eyes may tread a lover's maze,
But with such turns the voice to stray,
No talk untaught can find the way;
The tip no jewel needs to wear—
The tip is jewel of the ear.
But who those ruddy lips can miss
Which, blessèd, still themselves do kiss?
Rubies, cherries, and roses new,
In worth, in taste, in perfect hue,
Which never part, but that they show
Of precious pearl the double row,
The second sweetly-fencèd ward
Her heavenly-dewèd tongue to guard,
Whence never word in vain did flow.
Fair under these doth stately grow
The handle of this pleasant work,
The neck, in which strange graces lurk;
Such be, I think, the sumptuous towers
Which skill doth make in princes' bowers.
So good assay invites the eye
A little downward to espy
The lively cluster of her breasts,
Of Venus' babe the wanton nests,
Like pommels round of marble clear,
Where azured veins well-mixed appear,

With dearest tops of porphyry;
Betwixt these two a way doth lie,
A way more worthy Beauty's fame
Than that which bears the milky name.
This leads unto the joyous field
Which only still doth lilies yield,
But lilies such whose native smell
The Indian odors doth excel:
Waist it is called, for it doth waste
Men's lives until it be embraced.
There may one see, and yet not see,
Her ribs in white well-armèd be,
More white than Neptune's foamy face
When struggling rocks he would embrace.
In these delights the wandering thought
Might of each side astray be brought,
But that her navel doth unite
In curious circle busy sight,
A dainty seal of virgin-wax,
Where nothing but impression lacks.
The belly, then, glad sight doth fill,
Justly entitled Cupid's hill,
A hill most fit for such a master,
A spotless mine of alabaster,
Like alabaster fair and sleek,
But soft and supple, satin-like;
In that sweet seat the boy doth sport.
Loath I must leave his chief resort,
For such a use the world hath gotten
The best things still must be forgotten.
Yet never shall my song omit
Those thighs, for Ovid's song more fit,
Which flankèd with two sugared flanks,
Lift up her stately-swelling banks,
That Albion's cliffs in whiteness pass,
With haunches smooth as looking-glass.
But, bow all knees! Now of her knees

My tongue doth tell what fancy sees,
The knots of joy, the gems of love,
Whose motion makes all graces move,
Whose bows incaved doth yield such sight
Like cunning painter shadowing white.
The gartering-place with childlike sign
Shows easy print in metal fine,
But there again the flesh doth rise
In her brave calves like crystal skies,
Whose Atlas is a smallest small,
More white than whitest bone of whale;
There oft steals out that round clean foot,
This noble cedar's precious root,
In show and scent pale violets,
Whose step on earth all beauty sets.
But back unto her back, my Muse,
Where Leda's swan her feathers mews,
Along whose ridge such bones are met,
Like comfits round in marchpane set.
Her shoulders be like two white doves,
Perching within square royal rooves,
Which leaded are with silver skin,
Passing the hate-spot ermelin;
And thence those arms derivèd are—
The phoenix' wings be not so rare
For faultless length and stainless hue.
Ah, woe is me, my woes renew;
Now course doth lead me to her hand,
Of my first love the fatal band,
Where whiteness doth forever sit—
Nature herself enameled it;
For there with strange compact doth lie
Warm snow, moist pearl, soft ivory;
There fall those sapphire-colored brooks,
Which conduit-like, with curious crooks,
Sweet islands make in that sweet land.
As for the fingers of the hand,

The bloody shafts of Cupid's war,
With amethysts they headed are.
Thus hath each part his beauty's part;
But how the Graces do impart
To all her limbs a special grace,
Becoming every time and place,
Which doth even beauty beautify,
And most bewitch the wretched eye.
How all this is but a fair inn
Of fairer guest which dwells within,
Of whose high praise and praiseful bliss
Goodness the pen, heaven paper is,
The ink immortal fame doth lend.
As I begun so must I end:
No tongue can her perfections tell,
In whose each part all pens may dwell.

SIR PHILIP SIDNEY

the boy: Cupid
Ovid's song: see Marlowe's translation in Section 8
smallest small: her ankle
mews: moults
comfits: sweetmeats
marchpane: cake
ermelin: *i.e.*, ermine, whose fur is white in winter except for black tail-tip

≥ ≤

PUELLA MEA

Harun Omar and Master Hafiz
keep your dead beautiful ladies.
Mine is a little lovelier
than any of your ladies were.

In her perfectest array
my lady, moving in the day,
is a little stranger thing
than crisp Sheba with her king
in the morning wandering.
   Through the young and awkward hours
my lady perfectly moving,
through the new world scarce astir
my fragile lady wandering
in whose perishable poise
is the mystery of Spring
(with her beauty more than snow
dexterous and fugitive
my very frail lady drifting
distinctly, moving like a myth
in the uncertain morning, with
April feet like sudden flowers
and all her body filled with May)
—moving in the unskilful day
my lady utterly alive,
to me is a more curious thing
(a thing more nimble and complete)
than ever to Judea's king
were the shapely sharp cunning
and withal delirious feet
of the Princess Salomé
carefully dancing in the noise
Of Herod's silence, long ago.
If she a little turn her head
i know that i am wholly dead:
nor ever did on such a throat
the lips of Tristram slowly dote,
La beale Isoud whose leman was.
And if my lady look at me
(with her eyes which like two elves
incredibly amuse themselves)
with a look of færie,

perhaps a little suddenly
(as sometimes the improbable
beauty of my lady will)
—at her glance my spirit shies
rearing (as in the miracle
of a lady who had eyes
which the king's horses might not kill.)
 But should my lady smile, it were
a flower of so pure surprise
(it were so very new a flower,
a flower so frail, a flower so glad)
as trembling used to yield with dew
when the world was young and new
(a flower such as the world had
in Springtime when the world was mad
and Launcelot spoke to Guenever,
a flower which most heavy hung
with silence when the world was young
and Diarmid looked in Grania's eyes.)
 But should my lady's beauty play
at not speaking (sometimes as
it will) the silence of her face
doth immediately make
in my heart so great a noise,
as in the sharp and thirsty blood
of Paris would not all the Troys
of Helen's beauty: never did
Lord Jason (in impossible things
victorious impossibly)
so wholly burn, to undertake
Medea's rescuing eyes; nor he
when swooned the white egyptian day
who with Egypt's body lay.

Lovely as those ladies were
mine is a little lovelier.
And if she speak in her frail way,

it is wholly to bewitch
my smallest thought with a most swift
radiance wherein slowly drift
murmurous things divinely bright;
it is foolingly to smite
my spirit with the lithe free twitch
of scintillant space, with the cool writhe
of gloom truly which syncopate
some sunbeam's skilful fingerings;
it is utterly to lull
with foliate inscrutable
sweetness my soul obedient;
it is to stroke my being with
numbing forests frolicsome,
fleetly mystical, aroam
with keen creatures of idiom
(beings alert and innocent
very deftly upon which
indolent miracles impinge)
—it is distinctly to confute
my reason with the deep caress
of every most shy thing and mute,
it is to quell me with the twinge
of all living intense things.
    Never my soul so fortunate
is (past the luck of all dead men
and loving) as invisibly when
upon her palpable solitude
a furtive occult fragrance steals,
a gesture of immaculate
perfume—whereby (with fear aglow)
my soul is wont wholly to know
the poignant instantaneous fern
whose scrupulous enchanted fronds
toward all things intrinsic yearn,
the immanent subliminal
fern of her delicious voice

(of her voice which always dwells
beside the vivid magical
impetuous and utter ponds
of dream; and very secret food
its leaves inimitable find
beyond the white authentic springs,
beyond the sweet instinctive wells,
which make to flourish the minute
spontaneous meadow of her mind)
—the vocal fern, always which feels
the keen ecstatic actual tread
(and thereto perfectly responds)
of all things exquisite and dead,
all living things and beautiful.

(Caliph and king their ladies had
to love them and to make them glad,
when the world was young and mad,
in the city of Bagdad—
mine is a little lovelier
than any of those ladies were.)

Her body is most beauteous,
being for all things amorous
fashioned very curiously
of roses and of ivory.
The immaculate crisp head
is such as only certain dead
and careful painters love to use
for their youngest angels (whose
praising bodies in a row
between slow glories fleetly go.)
Upon a keen and lovely throat
the strangeness of her face doth float,
which in eyes and lips consists
—always upon the mouth there trysts
curvingly a fragile smile
which like a flower lieth (while

within the eyes is dimly heard
a wistful and precarious bird.)
Springing from fragrant shoulders small,
ardent, and perfectly withal
smooth to stroke and sweet to see
as a supple and young tree,
her slim lascivious arms alight
in skilful wrists which hint at flight
—my lady's very singular
and slenderest hands moreover are
(which as lilies smile and quail)
of all things perfect the most frail.

(Whoso rideth in the tale
of Chaucer knoweth many a pair
of companions blithe and fair;
who to walk with Master Gower
in Confessio doth prefer
shall not lack for beauty there,
nor he that will amaying go
with my lord Boccaccio—
whoso knocketh at the door
of Marie and of Maleore
findeth of ladies goodly store
whose beauty did in nothing err.
If to me there shall appear
than a rose more sweetly known,
more silently than a flower,
my lady naked in her hair—
i for those ladies nothing care
nor any lady dead and gone.)

Each tapering breast is firm and smooth
that in a lovely fashion doth
from my lady's body grow;
as morning may a lily know,
her petaled flesh doth entertain
the adroit blood's mysterious skein

(but like some passionate earlier
flower, the snow will oft utter,
whereof the year has perfect bliss—
for each breast a blossom is,
which being a little while caressed
its fragrance makes the lover blest.)
Her waist is a most tiny hinge
of flesh, a winsome thing and strange;
apt in my hand warmly to lie
it is a throbbing neck whereby
to grasp the belly's ample vase
(that urgent urn which doth amass
for whoso drinks, a dizzier wine
than should the grapes of heaven combine
with earth's madness)—'tis a gate
unto a palace intricate
(whereof the luscious pillars rise
which are her large and shapely thighs)
in whose dome the trembling bliss
of a kingdom wholly is.

   Beneath her thighs such legs are seen
as were the pride of the world's queen:
each is a verb, miraculous
inflected oral devious,
beneath the body's breathing noun
(moreover the delicious frown
of the grave great sensual knees
well might any monarch please.)
Each ankle is divinely shy;
as if for fear you would espy
the little distinct foot (if whose
very minuteness doth abuse
reason, why then the artificer
did most exquisitely err.)

When the world was like a song
heard behind a golden door,

poet and sage and caliph had
to love them and to make them glad
ladies with lithe eyes and long
(when the world was like a flower
Omar Hafiz and Harun
loved their ladies in the moon)
—fashioned very curiously
of roses and of ivory
if naked she appear to me
my flesh is an enchanted tree;
with her lips' most frail parting
my body hears the cry of Spring,
and with their frailest syllable
its leaves go crisp with miracle.

Love!—maker of my lady,
in that always beyond this
poem or any poem she
of whose body words are afraid
perfectly beautiful is,
forgive these words which i have made.
And never boast your dead beauties,
you greatest lovers in the world!
who with Grania strangely fled,
who with Egypt went to bed,
whom white-thighed Semiramis
put up her mouth to wholly kiss—
never boast your dead beauties,
mine being unto me sweeter
(of whose shy delicious glance
things which never more shall be,
perfect things of færie,
are intense inhabitants;
in whose warm superlative
body do distinctly live
all sweet cities passed away—
in her flesh at break of day

are the smells of Nineveh,
in her eyes when day is gone
are the cries of Babylon.)
Diarmid Paris and Solomon,
Omar Harun and Master Hafiz,
to me your ladies are all one—
keep your dead beautiful ladies.

Eater of all things lovely—Time!
upon whose watering lips the world
poises a moment (futile, proud,
a costly morsel of sweet tears)
gesticulates, and disappears—
of all dainties which do crowd
gaily upon oblivion
sweeter than any there is one;
to touch it is the fear of rhyme—
in life's very fragile hour
(when the world was like a tale
made of laughter and of dew,
was a flight, a flower, a flame,
was a tendril fleetly curled
upon frailness) used to stroll
(very slowly) one or two
ladies like flowers made,
softly used to wholly move
slender ladies made of dream
(in the lazy world and new
sweetly used to laugh and love
ladies with crisp eyes and frail,
in the city of Bagdad.)

Keep your dead beautiful ladies
Harun Omar and Master Hafiz.

E. E. CUMMINGS

Puella Mea: My Girl

❧ *NOTES* ❦

I don't know whose foot is more enchanting—Ben's or the lady's—
in "Here she was wont to go! And here! And here!" The nine lines
comprise the entire first scene of Act I of *The Sad Shepherd; or, A Tale
of Robin Hood,* published for the first time in the 1640 folio of Jonson's *Works.* They are spoken by Aeglamour, the sad shepherd of the
title.

The charming "Madrigal" that follows Herrick's poem is from *A
Poetical Rhapsody,* 1602.

John Cournos was a member of the Pound circle in Kensington and
is represented in the famous *Des Imagistes* anthology. His poem in this
section is from *With Hey, Ho . . . and The Man With the Spats,*
published in 1963. From the same volume:

A VALENTINE

I am three score—and twenty,
So what's to be done, my dear?
I must resign love's plenty
And say my prayers, I fear.

Too bad so late I met you,
Too late for love, my sweet,
If I were only twenty-two
I'd wed you *tout de suite.*

I've gathered aged wisdom,
Surfeit of sense and lore,
But I'd give away my kingdom
To be only twenty-four!

He will be eighty-five when this book appears.

Prior's mirror poem is an adaptation from Plato in the *Greek Anthology* (VI, 1).

Surrey's "In Praise of His Love" has another title, by an earlier editor: "Wherein he reproveth them that compare their ladies with his."
The repetition of "I" in the third stanza is not unusual; in Marlowe's
translation of Ovid's second elegy it adds to the charm of the line:

> Lo, I confess I am thy captive, I,
> And hold my conquer'd hands for thee to tie.

Donne has also used it—see the closing lines of "On His Mistress,"
p. 154.

Sidney's and Cummings' elaborate descriptions of their ladies have a
counterpart in Spenser's "Epithalamion," stanza ten:

> Tell me, ye merchants' daughters, did ye see
> So fair a creature in your town before,
> So sweet, so lovely, and so mild as she,
> Adorned with beauty's grace and virtue's store:
> Her goodly eyes like sapphires shining bright,
> Her forehead ivory white,
> Her cheeks like apples which the sun hath rudded,
> Her lips like cherries charming men to bite,
> Her breast like to a bowl of cream uncrudded,
> Her paps like lilies budded,
> Her snowy neck like to a marble tower,
> And all her body like a palace fair,
> Ascending up with many a stately stair
> To honor's seat and chastity's sweet bower.

But the "Song of Solomon" precedes them all:

> Behold, thou art fair, my love; behold, thou art fair; thou hast doves'
> eyes within thy locks: thy hair is as a flock of goats that appear from
> Mount Gilead.
>   Thy teeth are like a flock of sheep that are even shorn, which came
> up from the washing; whereof every one bear twins, and none is barren
> among them.
>   Thy lips are like a thread of scarlet, and thy speech is comely: thy
> temples are like a piece of a pomegranate within thy locks.
>   Thy neck is like the tower of David builded for an armoury, whereon
> there hang a thousand bucklers, all shields of mighty men.
>   Thy two breasts are like two young roes that are twins, which feed
> among the lilies. *Chap. 4.*

10.

People

10. PEOPLE

MIRANDA'S WONDER

O brave new world,
That has such people in't!

WILLIAM SHAKESPEARE

ELIZABETHAN WEEK-END

Faustinus, Sextus, Cinna, Ponticus,
With Gella, Lesbia, Thais, Rhodope,
Rode all to Staines for no cause serious,
But for their mirth, and for their lechery.
Scarce were they settled in their lodging when
Wenches with wenches, men with men, fell out,
Men with their wenches, wenches with their men,
Which straight dissolves this ill-assembled rout.
But since the devil brought them thus together,
To my discoursing thoughts it is a wonder,
Why presently as soon as they came thither,
The selfsame devil did them part asunder.
  Doubtless it seems it was a foolish devil
  That thus did part them ere they did some evil.

SIR JOHN DAVIES

PHYLLIS, OR THE PROGRESS OF LOVE

Desponding Phyllis was endued
With ev'ry talent of a prude;
She trembled when a man drew near,
Salute her, and she turned her ear;
If o'er against her you were placed
She durst not look above your waist;
She'd rather take you to her bed
Than let you see her dress her head.
In church your heard her through the crowd
Repeat the absolution loud;
In church, secure behind her fan,
She durst behold that monster, man;
There practiced how to place her head,
And bit her lips to make them red,
Or on the mat devoutly kneeling
Would lift her eyes up to the ceiling,
And heave her bosom unaware
For neigh'bring beaux to see it bare.

At length a lucky lover came,
And found admittance to the dame.
Suppose all parties now agreed,
The writings drawn, the lawyer feed,
The vicar and the ring bespoke:
Guess how could such a match be broke.
See, then, what mortals place their bliss in!
Next morn betimes the bride was missin',
The mother screamed, the father chid,
Where can this idle wench be hid?
No news of Phyl. The bridegroom came,
And thought his bride had skulked for shame,
Because her father used to say
The girl had such a bashful way.

Now John, the butler, must be sent
To learn the way that Phyllis went;
The groom was wished to saddle 'Crop,'

For John must neither 'light nor stop,
But find her wheresoe'er she fled,
And bring her back, alive or dead.
See here again the devil to do:
For, truly, John was missing, too,
The horse and pillion both were gone;
Phyllis, it seems, had fled with John.
Old madam, who went up to find
What papers Phyl had left behind,
A letter on the toilet sees
'To my much honored Father, these—'
('Tis always done, romances tell us,
When daughters run away with fellows)
Filled with the choicest commonplaces,
By others used in the like cases:
That, long ago, a fortune-teller
Exactly said what now befell her,
And in a glass had made her see
A serving-man of low degree;
It was her fate, must be forgiven,
For marriages are made in heaven;
His pardon begged, but to be plain,
She'd do 't if 'twere to do again;
Thank God, 'twas neither shame nor sin,
For John was come of honest kin;
Love never thinks of rich and poor—
She'd beg with John from door to door;
Forgive her, if it be a crime,
She'll never do 't another time;
She ne'er before in all her life
Once disobeyed him, maid nor wife.
One argument she summed up all in—
The thing was done and past recallin',
And therefore hoped she would recover
His favor, when his passion's over;
She valued not what others thought her,
And was—his most obedient daughter.

Fair maidens all, attend the Muse
Who now the wand'ring pair pursues:
Away they rode in homely sort,
Their journey long, their money short,
The loving couple well bemired,
The horse and both the riders tired,
Their victuals bad, their lodging worse;
Phyl cried, and John began to curse.
Phyl wished that she had strained a limb
When first she ventured out with him;
John wished that he had broke a leg
When first for her he quitted Peg.

But what adventures more befell 'em
The Muse has now not time to tell 'em:
How Johnny wheedled, threatened, fawned,
Till Phyllis all her trinkets pawned;
How oft she broke her marriage vows
In kindness to maintain her spouse,
Till swains unwholesome spoiled the trade,
For now the surgeons must be paid,
To whom those perquisites are gone,
In Christian justice due to John.

When food and raiment now grew scarce
Fate put a period to the farce,
And with exact poetic justice:
For John is landlord, Phyllis hostess.
They keep at Staines the old *Blue Boar,*
Are cat and dog, and rogue and whore.

JONATHAN SWIFT

pillion: cushion attached to hinder part of saddle
toilet: dressing table

THE OLD AND YOUNG COURTIER

An old song made by an aged old pate,
Of an old worshipful gentleman, who had a great estate,
That kept a brave old house at a bountiful rate,
And an old porter to relieve the poor at his gate,
    Like an old courtier of the Queen's,
    And the Queen's old courtier.

With an old lady, whose anger one word assuages;
They every quarter paid their old servants their wages,
And never knew what belonged to coachman, footmen, nor pages,
But kept twenty old fellows with blue coats and badges;
    Like an old courtier of the Queen's,
    And the Queen's old courtier.

With an old study filled full of learnèd old books,
With an old reverend chaplain, you might know him by his looks,
With an old buttery hatch quite worn off the hooks,
And an old kitchen, that maintained half a dozen old cooks;
    Like an old courtier of the Queen's,
    And the Queen's old courtier.

With an old hall hung about with pikes, guns and bows,
With old swords, and bucklers, that had borne many shrewd blows,
And an old frieze coat to cover his worship's trunk hose,
And a cup of old sherry, to comfort his copper nose;
    Like an old courtier of the Queen's,
    And the Queen's old courtier.

With a good old fashion, when Christmas was come,
To call in all his neighbors with bagpipe and drum,
With good cheer enough to furnish every old room,
And old liquor able to make a cat speak, and man dumb,
    Like an old courtier of the Queen's,
    And the Queen's old courtier.

With an old falconer, huntsman, and a kennel of hounds,
That never hawked, nor hunted, but in his own grounds,

Who, like a wise man, kept himself within his own bounds,
And when he died gave every child a thousand pounds,
    Like an old courtier of the Queen's,
    And the Queen's old courtier.

But to his eldest son his house and lands he assigned,
Charging him in his will to keep the old bountiful mind,
To be good to his old tenants, and to his neighbors be kind;
But in the ensuing ditty you shall hear how he was inclined,
    Like a young courtier of the King's,
    And the King's young courtier.

Like a flourishing young gallant, newly come to his land,
Who keeps a brace of painted madams at his command,
And takes up a thousand pound upon his father's land,
And gets drunk in a tavern, till he can neither go nor stand,
    Like a young courtier of the King's,
    And the King's young courtier.

With a new-fangled lady, that is dainty, nice, and spare,
Who never knew what belonged to good housekeeping, or care,
Who buys gaudy-colored fans to play with wanton air,
And seven or eight different dressings of other women's hair;
    Like a young courtier of the King's,
    And the King's young courtier.

With a new-fashioned hall, built where the old one stood,
Hung round with new pictures, that do the poor no good,
With a fine marble chimney, wherein burns neither coal nor wood,
And a new smooth shovel-board, whereon victuals ne'er stood;
    Like a young courtier of the King's,
    And the King's young courtier.

With a new study, stuffed full of pamphlets and plays,
And a new chaplain, that swears faster than he prays,
With a new buttery hatch, that opens once in four or five days,
And a new French cook, to devise fine kickshaws and toys;
    Like a young courtier of the King's,
    And the King's young courtier.

With a new fashion, when Christmas is drawing on,
On a new journey to London straight we all must begone,
And leave none to keep house, but our new porter John,
Who relieves the poor with a thump on the back with a stone;
  Like a young courtier of the King's,
  And the King's young courtier.

With a new gentleman-usher, whose carriage is complete,
With a new coachman, footmen, and pages to carry up the meat,
With a waiting-gentlewoman, whose dressing is very neat,
Who when her lady has dined, lets the servants not eat;
  Like a young courtier of the King's,
  And the King's young courtier.

With new titles of honor bought with his father's old gold,
For which sundry of his ancestors' old manors are sold;
And this is the course most of our new gallants hold,
Which makes that good house-keeping is now grown so old,
  Among the young courtiers of the King's,
  Or the King's young courtiers.

ANON.

TWO EPIGRAMS

ANTIQUARY

If in his study he hath so much care
To hang all old, strange things up, let his wife beware.

MANLINESS

Thou call'st me effeminate, for I love women's joys;
I call not thee manly, though thou follow boys.

JOHN DONNE

LULLABY

Sing lullaby, as women do,
   Wherewith they bring their babes to rest,
And lullaby can I sing, too,
   As womanly as can the best.
With lullaby they still the child,
And, if I be not much beguiled,
Full many wanton babes have I
Which must be stilled with lullaby.

First, lullaby my youthful years,
   It is now time to go to bed,
For crooked age and hoary hairs
   Have won the haven within my head.
With lullaby, then, youth be still,
With lullaby content thy will;
Since courage quails and comes behind,
Go sleep, and so beguile thy mind.

Next, lullaby my gazing eyes,
   Which wonted were to gaze apace,
For every glass may now suffice
   To show the furrows in my face.
With lullaby, then, wink awhile,
With lullaby your looks beguile;
Let no fair face, nor beauty bright,
Entice you eft with vain delight.

And lullaby my wanton will—
   Let reason's rule now rein thy thought,
Since all too late I find by skill
   How dear I have thy fancies bought.
With lullaby now take thine ease,
With lullaby thy doubts appease;
For trust to this, if thou be still,
My body shall obey thy will.

Eke lullaby my loving boy;
  My little Robin, take thy rest;
Since age is cold, and nothing coy,
  Keep close thy coin, for so is best.
With lullaby be thou content,
With lullaby thy lusts relent;
Let others pay which have mo pence—
Thou art too poor for such expense.

Thus lullaby my youth, mine eyes,
  My will, my ware, and all that was;
I can no more delays devise,
  But welcome pain, let pleasure pass.
With lullaby now take your leave,
With lullaby your dreams deceive,
And when you rise with waking eye,
Remember then this lullaby.

GEORGE GASCOIGNE

eft: again
mo: more

᠀ ᠁

RESOLUTION IN FOUR SONNETS, OF A POETICAL QUESTION PUT TO ME BY A FRIEND, CONCERNING FOUR RURAL SISTERS

I

Alice is tall and upright as a pine,
White as blanched almonds, or the falling snow,
Sweet as are damask roses when they blow,
And doubtless fruitful as the swelling vine.

Ripe to be cut, and ready to be pressed,
Her full cheeked beauties very well appear,
And a year's fruit she loses ev'ry year,
Wanting a man t' improve her to the best.

Full fain she would be husbanded, and yet,
Alas! she cannot a fit lab'rer get
To cultivate her to her own content:

Fain would she be (God wot) about her task,
And yet (forsooth) she is too proud to ask,
And (which is worse) too modest to consent.

II

Marg'ret of humbler stature by the head
Is (as it oft falls out with yellow hair)
Than her fair sister, yet so much more fair,
As her pure white is better mixed with red.

This, hotter than the other ten to one,
Longs to be put unto her mother's trade,
And loud proclaims she lives too long a maid,
Wishing for one t' untie her virgin zone.

She finds virginity a kind of ware
That's very very troublesome to bear,
And being gone, she thinks will ne'er be missed:

And yet withal the girl has so much grace,
To call for help I know she wants the face,
Though asked, I know not how she would resist.

III

Mary is black, and taller than the last,
Yet equal in perfection and desire,
To the one's melting snow, and t' other's fire,
As with whose black their fairness is defaced.

She pants as much for love as th' other two,
But she so virtuous is, or else so wise,

That she will win or will not love a prize,
And but upon good terms will never do.

Therefore who her will conquer ought to be
At least as full of love and wit as she,
Or he shall ne'er gain favor at her hands:

Nay, though he have a pretty store of brains,
Shall only have his labor for his pains,
Unless he offer more than she demands.

IV
Martha is not so tall, nor yet so fair
As any of the other lovely three,
Her chiefest grace is poor simplicity,
Yet were the rest away, she were a star.

She's fair enough, only she wants the art
To set her beauties off as they can do,
And that's the cause she ne'er heard any woo,
Nor ever yet made conquest of a heart.

And yet her blood's as boiling as the best,
Which, pretty soul, does so disturb her rest,
And makes her languish so, she's fit to die:

Poor thing, I doubt she still must lie alone,
For being like to be attacked by none,
Sh'as no more wit to ask than to deny.

CHARLES COTTON

PORTRAIT OF A LADY
In the Exhibition of The Royal Academy

What are you, Lady?—naught is here
  To tell us of your name or story;
To claim the gazer's smile or tear,
  To dub you Whig, or damn you Tory.

It is beyond a poet's skill
    To form the slightest notion, whether
We e'er shall walk through one quadrille,
    Or look upon one moon together.

You're very pretty!—all the world
    Are talking of your bright brow's splendor,
And of your locks, so softly curled,
    And of your hands, so white and slender:
Some think you're blooming in Bengal;
    Some say you're blowing in the city;
Some know you're nobody at all;
    I only feel, you're very pretty.

But bless my heart! it's very wrong:
    You're making all our belles ferocious;
Anne 'never saw a chin so long';
    And Laura thinks your dress 'atrocious';
And Lady Jane, who now and then
    Is taken for the village steeple,
Is sure you can't be four feet ten,
    And 'wonders at the taste of people.'

Soon pass the praises of a face;
    Swift fades the very best vermilion;
Fame rides a most prodigious pace;
    Oblivion follows on the pillion;
And all, who, in these sultry rooms,
    Today have stared, and pushed, and fainted,
Will soon forget your pearls and plumes,
    As if they never had been painted.

You'll be forgotten—as old debts
    By persons who are used to borrow;
Forgotten—as the sun that sets,
    When shines a new one on the morrow;
Forgotten—like the luscious peach,
    That blessed the school-boy last September;

Forgotten—like a maiden speech,
    Which all men praise, but none remember.

Yet, ere you sink into the stream,
    That whelms alike sage, saint, and martyr,
And soldier's sword, and minstrel's theme,
    And Canning's wit, and Gratton's charter,
Here of the fortunes of your youth
    My fancy weaves her dim conjectures,
Which have, perhaps, as much of truth
    As passion's vows, or Cobbett's lectures.

Was 't in the north or in the south,
    That summer-breezes rocked your cradle?
And had you in your baby mouth
    A wooden or a silver ladle?
And was your first, unconscious sleep,
    By brownie banned, or blessed by fairy?
And did you wake to laugh or weep?
    And were you christened Maud or Mary?

And was your father called 'your grace'?
    And did he bet at Ascot races?
And did he chat at common-place?
    And did he fill a score of places?
And did your lady-mother's charms
    Consist in picklings, broilings, bastings?
Or did she prate about the arms
    Her brave forefathers wore at Hastings?

Where were you 'finished'? tell me where!
    Was it at Chelsea, or at Chiswick?
Had you the ordinary share
    Of books and backboard, harp and physic?
And did they bid you banish pride,
    And mind your oriental tinting?
And did you learn how Dido died,
    And who found out the art of printing?

And are you fond of lanes and brooks,
    A votary of the sylvan muses?
Or do you con the little books
    Which Baron Brougham and Vaux diffuses?
Or do you love to knit and sew,
    The fashionable world's Arachne?
Or do you canter down the Row,
    Upon a very long-tailed hackney?

And do you love your brother James?
    And do you pet his mares and setters?
And have your friends romantic names?
    And do you write them long, long letters?
And are you—since the world began
    All women are—a little spiteful?
And don't you dote on Malibran?
    And don't you think Tom Moore delightful?

I see they've brought you flowers today,
    Delicious food for eyes and noses;
But carelessly you turn away
    From all the pinks, and all the roses;
Say, is that fond look sent in search
    Of one whose look as fondly answers?
And is he, fairest, in the Church,
    Or is he—ain't he—in the Lancers?

And is your love a motley page
    Of black and white, half joy, half sorrow?
Are you to wait till you're of age?
    Or are you to be his to-morrow?
Or do they bid you, in their scorn,
    Your pure and sinless flame to smother?
Is he so very meanly born?
    Or are you married to another?

Whate'er you are, at last, adieu!
    I think it is your bounden duty

To let the rhymes I coin for you,
  Be prized by all who prize your beauty.
From you I seek nor gold nor fame;
  From you I fear no cruel strictures;
I wish some girls that I could name
  Were half as silent as their pictures!

WINTHROP MACKWORTH PRAED

PORTRAIT D'UNE FEMME

Your mind and you are our Sargasso sea,
London has swept about you this score years
And bright ships left you this or that in fee:
Ideas, old gossip, oddments of all things,
Strange spars of knowledge and dimmed wares of price.
Great minds have sought you—lacking someone else.
You have been second always. Tragical?
No. You preferred it to the usual thing:
One dull man, dulling and uxorious,
One average mind—with one thought less each year.
Oh, you are patient, I have seen you sit
Hours, where something might have floated up.
And now you pay one. Yes, you richly pay.
You are a person of some interest, one comes to you
And takes strange gain away:
Trophies fished up; some curious suggestion;
Fact that leads nowhere; and a tale or two,
Pregnant with mandrakes, or with something else
That might prove useful and yet never proves,
That never fits a corner or shows use,
Or finds its hour upon the loom of days:
The tarnished, gaudy, wonderful old work;
Idols and ambergris and rare inlays,

These are your riches, your great store; and yet
For all this sea-hoard of deciduous things,
Strange woods half sodden, and new brighter stuff:
In the slow float of differing light and deep,
No! there is nothing! In the whole and all,
Nothing that's quite your own.
        Yet this is you.

EZRA POUND

A LIGHT WOMAN

So far as our story approaches the end,
   Which do you pity the most of us three?—
My friend, or the mistress of my friend
   With her wanton eyes, or me?

My friend was already too good to lose,
   And seemed in the way of improvement yet,
When she crossed his path with her hunting-noose,
   And over him drew her net.

When I saw him tangled in her toils,
   A shame, said I, if she adds just him
To her nine-and-ninety other spoils,
   The hundredth for a whim!

And before my friend be wholly hers,
   How easy to prove to him, I said,
An eagle's the game her pride prefers,
   Though she snaps at a wren instead!

So, I gave her eyes my own eyes to take,
   My hand sought hers as in earnest need,
And round she turned for my noble sake,
   And gave me herself indeed.

The eagle am I, with my fame in the world,
  The wren is he, with his maiden face.
—You look away and your lip is curled?
  Patience, a moment's space!

For see, my friend goes shaking and white;
  He eyes me as the basilisk:
I have turned, it appears, his day to night,
  Eclipsing his sun's disk.

And I did it, he thinks, as a very thief:
  'Though I love her—that, he comprehends—
One should master one's passions, (love, in chief)
  And be loyal to one's friends!'

And she,—she lies in my hand as tame
  As a pear late basking over a wall;
Just a touch to try and off it came;
  'Tis mine,—can I let it fall?

With no mind to eat it, that's the worst!
  Were it thrown in the road, would the case assist?
'T was quenching a dozen blue-flies' thirst
  When I gave its stalk a twist.

And I,—what I seem to my friend, you see:
  What I soon shall seem to his love, you guess:
What I seem to myself, do you ask of me?
  No hero, I confess.

'Tis an awkward thing to play with souls,
  And matter enough to save one's own:
Yet think of my friend, and the burning coals
  He played with for bits of stone!

One likes to show the truth for the truth;
  That the woman was light is very true:
But suppose she says,—Never mind that youth!
  What wrong have I done to you?

Well, anyhow, here the story stays,
    So far at least as I understand;
And, Robert Browning, you writer of plays,
    Here's a subject made to your hand!

ROBERT BROWNING

≥ ≤

I AM A PARCEL OF VAIN STRIVINGS TIED

I am a parcel of vain strivings tied
    By a chance bond together,
Dangling this way and that, their links
    Were made so loose and wide,
        Methinks,
    For milder weather.

A bunch of violets without their roots,
    And sorrel intermixed,
Encircled by a wisp of straw
    Once coiled about their shoots,
        The law
    By which I'm fixed.

A nosegay which Time clutched from out
    Those fair Elysian fields,
With weeds and broken stems, in haste,
    Doth make the rabble rout
        That waste
    The day he yields.

And here I bloom for a short hour unseen,
    Drinking my juices up,
With no root in the land
    To keep my branches green,
        But stand
    In a bare cup.

Some tender buds were left upon my stem
    In mimicry of life,
  But ah! the children will not know,
    Till time has withered them,
        The woe
    With which they're rife.

But now I see I was not plucked for naught,
    And after in life's vase
  Of glass set while I might survive,
    But by a kind hand brought
        Alive
    To a strange place.

That stock thus thinned will soon redeem its hours,
    And by another year,
  Such as God knows, with freer air,
    More fruits and fairer flowers
        Will bear,
    While I droop here.

HENRY DAVID THOREAU

MINIVER CHEEVY

Miniver Cheevy, child of scorn,
  Grew lean while he assailed the seasons;
He wept that he was ever born,
  And he had reasons.

Miniver loved the days of old
  When swords were bright and steeds were prancing;
The vision of a warrior bold
  Would set him dancing.

Miniver sighed for what was not,
    And dreamed, and rested from his labors;
He dreamed of Thebes and Camelot,
    And Priam's neighbors.

Miniver mourned the ripe renown
    That made so many a name so fragrant;
He mourned Romance, now on the town,
    And Art, a vagrant.

Miniver loved the Medici,
    Albeit he had never seen one;
He would have sinned incessantly
    Could he have been one.

Miniver cursed the commonplace
    And eyed a khaki suit with loathing;
He missed the medieval grace
    Of iron clothing.

Miniver scorned the gold he sought,
    But sore annoyed was he without it;
Miniver thought, and thought, and thought,
    And thought about it.

Miniver Cheevy, born too late,
    Scratched his head and went on thinking;
Miniver coughed, and called it fate,
    And kept on drinking.

EDWIN ARLINGTON ROBINSON

TWO FIGURES IN DENSE VIOLET NIGHT

I had as lief be embraced by the porter at the hotel
As to get no more from the moonlight
Than your moist hand.

Be the voice of night and Florida in my ear.
Use dusky words and dusky images.
Darken your speech.

Speak, even, as if I did not hear you speaking,
But spoke for you perfectly in my thoughts,
Conceiving words,

As the night conceives the sea-sounds in silence,
And out of their droning sibilants makes
A serenade.

Say, puerile, that the buzzards crouch on the ridge-pole
And sleep with one eye watching the stars fall
Below Key West.

Say that the palms are clear in a total blue,
Are clear and are obscure; that it is night;
That the moon shines.

WALLACE STEVENS

THE CYPRESS

I dug, beneath the cypress shade,
    What well might seem an elfin's grave;
And every pledge in earth I laid,
    That erst thy false affection gave.

I pressed them down the sod beneath;
    I placed one mossy stone above;
And twined the rose's fading wreath
    Around the sepulcher of love.

Frail as thy love, the flowers were dead,
    Ere yet the evening sun was set;
But years shall see the cypress spread,
    Immutable as my regret.

THOMAS LOVE PEACOCK

cypress: common in graveyards; also, emblem
of mourning

LA FIGLIA CHE PIANGE

O quam te memorem virgo. . . .

Stand on the highest pavement of the stair—
Lean on a garden urn—
Weave, weave the sunlight in your hair—
Clasp your flowers to you with a pained surprise—
Fling them to the ground and turn
With a fugitive resentment in your eyes:
But weave, weave the sunlight in your hair.

So I would have had him leave,
So I would have had her stand and grieve,
So he would have left
As the soul leaves the body torn and bruised,
As the mind deserts the body it has used.
I should find
Some way incomparably light and deft,
Some way we both should understand,
Simple and faithless as a smile and shake of the hand.

She turned away, but with the autumn weather
Compelled my imagination many days,
Many days and many hours:
Her hair over her arms and her arms full of flowers.
And I wonder how they should have been together!
I should have lost a gesture and a pose.
Sometimes these cogitations still amaze
The troubled midnight and the noon's repose.

T. S. ELIOT

La Figlia Che Piange: The Mourning Girl (but literally,
  "Daughter")
O quam te memorem virgo: "By what name should I call
  thee, O maiden?" Aeneas to his mother Venus; Virgil, *The
  Aeneid,* Book I

⊁ NOTES ⊱

The work in this section, taken as a whole, differs from that of the other sections because of a preponderance of poems that—strictly speaking—fall into the category of verse; but it is verse so skilfully fashioned as to take on some of the attributes of poetry. As for the subject matter, perhaps a commentary on the whole may be found in the chorus to "The Secular Masque" of Dryden, itself a masterpiece of versification:

> All, all, of a piece throughout;
> Thy chase had a beast in view;
> Thy wars brought nothing about;
> Thy lovers were all untrue.
> 'Tis well an old age is out,
> And time to begin a new.

Sir John Davies is the same whose epigrams were published with Marlowe's translations from Ovid (see notes to Section 1). It is curious to find that the place near London to which his eightsome resorted in the age of Elizabeth I is named by Swift in the poem that follows.

"The Old and Young Courtier" is a charming evocation of past and changing times; in the second half, the behavior of the young man resembles that of Sir John Lade, whose coming of age is celebrated in Samuel Johnson's "Long-Expected One-and-Twenty" (Section 6).

Gascoigne's patron was Arthur, Lord Grey of Wilton, the employer and patron of Spenser. He appears to have been a robust character, from charges made against him in 1572:

Item, he is a defamed person and noted as well for manslaughter as for other great crimes.
Item, he is a common rhymer and a deviser of slanderous pasquelles [pasquinades: lampoons] against divers persons of great calling.
Item, he is a notorious ruffian and especially noted to be both a spy, an atheist and a godless person.

The same charges were made against Marlowe some twenty years later, before he was murdered. There is nothing common about Gascoigne's poems, and he holds the honor of being one of the first writers of blank verse drama: *Jocasta,* "translated and digested into act" from Euripides, and the first Greek drama in English.

All three of the famous American expatriates—Henry James, T. S. Eliot, and Ezra Pound—wrote portraits of ladies; perhaps the poets' titles were suggested by the title of James' novel. The contrast between Praed's and Pound's ladies is very marked—the one not only unknown, but with all the attributes to turn a gazer into a gallant; the other, older, presumably a hostess, known, and possibly a bore. The movement in each poem seems appropriate to the subject. Praed was a felicitous writer of society verse; Austin Dobson termed him the "laureate-elect" of good society. During his brief life his poems appeared only in periodicals; in 1864 they were collected in two volumes, with a memoir by the Rev. Derwent Coleridge.

11.

Places

11. PLACES

ROMANCE

When I was but thirteen or so
  I went into a golden land,
Chimborazo, Cotopaxi
  Took me by the hand.

My father died, my brother too,
  They passed like fleeting dreams.
I stood where Popocatapetl
  In the sunlight gleams.

I dimly heard the Master's voice
  And boys far-off at play,
Chimborazo, Cotopaxi
  Had stolen me away.

I walked in a great golden dream
  To and fro from school—
Shining Popocatapetl
  The dusty streets did rule.

I walked home with a gold dark boy
  And never a word I'd say,
Chimborazo, Cotopaxi
  Had taken my speech away:

I gazed entranced upon his face
  Fairer than any flower—
O shining Popocatapetl
  It was thy magic hour:

The houses, people, traffic seemed
  Thin fading dreams by day,
Chimborazo, Cotopaxi
  They had stolen my soul away!

WALTER JAMES TURNER

❧ ❧

PARIS

Paris; this April sunset completely utters
utters serenely silently a cathedral
before whose upward lean magnificent face
the streets turn young with rain,

spiral acres of bloated rose
coiled within cobalt miles of sky
yield to and heed
the mauve
      of twilight (who slenderly descends,
daintily carrying in her eyes the dangerous first stars)
people move love hurry in a gently

arriving gloom and
see! (the new moon
fills abruptly with sudden silver
these torn pockets of lame and begging colour) while
there and here the lithe indolent prostitute
Night argues

with certain houses

E. E. CUMMINGS

ADLESTROP

Yes. I remember Adlestrop—
The name, because one afternoon
Of heat the express-train drew up there
Unwontedly. It was late June.

The steam hiss'd. Some one clear'd his throat.
No one left and no one came
On the bare platform. What I saw
Was Adlestrop—only the name

And willows, willow-herb, and grass,
And meadowsweet, and haycocks dry,
No whit less still and lonely fair
Than the high cloudlets in the sky.

And for that minute a blackbird sang
Close by, and round him, mistier,
Farther and farther, all the birds
Of Oxfordshire and Gloucestershire.

EDWARD THOMAS

PERSEPOLIS

MENAPHON

Your majesty shall shortly have your wish,
And ride in triumph through Persepolis.

TAMBURLAINE

And ride in triumph through Persepolis?
Is it not brave to be a king, Techelles?
Usumcasane and Theridamas,
It is not passing brave to be a king,
And ride in triumph through Persepolis?

TECHELLES

O, my lord, 'tis sweet and full of pomp.

CHRISTOPHER MARLOWE

THE OLD SHIPS

I have seen old ships sail like swans asleep
Beyond the village which men still call Tyre,
With leaden age o'ercargoed, dipping deep
For Famagusta and the hidden sun
That rings black Cyprus with a lake of fire;
And all those ships were certainly so old
Who knows how oft with squat and noisy gun,
Questing brown slaves or Syrian oranges,
The pirate Genoese
Hell-raked them till they rolled
Blood, water, fruit and corpses up the hold.
But now through friendly seas they softly run,
Painted the mid-sea blue or shore-sea green,
Still patterned with the vine and grapes in gold.

But I have seen,
Pointing her shapely shadows from the dawn
And image tumbled on a rose-swept bay,
A drowsy ship of some yet older day;
And, wonder's breath indrawn,
Thought I—who knows—who knows—but in that same
(Fished up beyond Aeaea, patched up new
—Stern painted brighter blue—)
That talkative, bald-headed seaman came
(Twelve patient comrades sweating at the oar)
From Troy's doom-crimson shore,
And with great lies about his wooden horse
Set the crew laughing, and forgot his course.

It was so old a ship—who knows, who knows?
—And yet so beautiful, I watched in vain
To see the mast burst open with a rose,
And the whole deck put on its leaves again.

JAMES ELROY FLECKER

ON THE EXTINCTION
OF THE VENETIAN REPUBLIC

Once did she hold the gorgeous East in fee,
And was the safeguard of the West: the worth
Of Venice did not fall below her birth,
Venice, the eldest child of Liberty.
She was a maiden city, bright and free;
No guile seduced, no force could violate;
And when she took unto herself a mate,
She must espouse the everlasting Sea.
And what if she had seen those glories fade,
Those titles vanish, and that strength decay;
Yet shall some tribute of regret be paid
When her long life hath reached its final day;
Men are we, and must grieve when even the shade
Of that which once was great is passed away.

WILLIAM WORDSWORTH

❧ ☙

ROME

At the Pyramid of Cestius Near the
Graves of Shelley and Keats

Who, then, was Cestius,
    And what is he to me?—
Amid thick thoughts and memories multitudinous
    One thought alone brings he.

    I can recall no word
    Of anything he did;
For me he is a man who died and was interred
    To leave a pyramid

Whose purpose was exprest
Not with its first design,
Nor till, far down in Time, beside it found their rest
Two countrymen of mine.

Cestius in life, maybe,
Slew, breathed out threatening;
I know not. This I know: in death all silently
He does a finer thing,

In beckoning pilgrim feet
With marble finger high
To where, by shadowy wall and history-haunted street,
Those matchless singers lie. . . .

—Say, then, he lived and died
That stones which bear his name
Should mark, through Time, where two immortal Shades abide;
It is an ample fame.

THOMAS HARDY

OZYMANDIAS

I met a traveller from an antique land
Who said: Two vast and trunkless legs of stone
Stand in the desert. Near them on the sand
Half sunk, a shatter'd visage lies, whose frown
And wrinkled lip and sneer of cold command
Tell that its sculptor well those passions read
Which yet survive, stamp'd on these lifeless things,
The hand that mock'd them and the heart that fed.
And on the pedestal these words appear,
'My name is Ozymandias, king of kings:
Look on my works, ye Mighty and despair!'
Nothing beside remains. Round the decay
Of that colossal wreck, boundless and bare,
The lone and level sands stretch far away.

PERCY BYSSHE SHELLEY

SUNDAY EVENING IN THE COMMON

Look, on the topmost branches of the world
The blossoms of the myriad stars are thick;
Over the huddled rows of stone and brick
A few sad wisps of empty smoke are curled,
Like ghosts languid and sick.

One breathless moment now the city's moaning
Fades, and the endless streets seem vague and dim.
There is no sound around the whole world's rim,
Save in the distance a small band is droning
Some desolate old hymn.

Van Wyck, how often have we been together
When this same moment made all mysteries clear:
The infinite stars that brood above us here,
And the gray city in the soft June weather,
So tawdry and so dear.

JOHN HALL WHEELOCK

Van Wyck: Van Wyck Brooks

MY LOST YOUTH

Often I think of the beautiful town
    That is seated by the sea;
Often in thought go up and down
The pleasant streets of that dear old town,
    And my youth comes back to me.
        And a verse of a Lapland song
        Is haunting my memory still:
        'A boy's will is the wind's will,
And the thoughts of youth are long, long thoughts.'

I can see the shadowy lines of its trees,
    And catch, in sudden gleams,
The sheen of the far-surrounding seas,
And islands that were the Hesperides
    Of all my boyish dreams.
        And the burden of that old song,
        It murmurs and whispers still:
        'A boy's will is the wind's will,
And the thoughts of youth are long, long thoughts.'

I remember the black wharves and the slips,
    And the sea-tides tossing free;
And Spanish sailors with bearded lips,
And the beauty and mystery of the ships,
    And the magic of the sea.
        And the voice of that wayward song
        Is singing and saying still:
        'A boy's will is the wind's will,
And the thoughts of youth are long, long thoughts.'

I remember the gleams and glooms that dart
    Across the schoolboy's brain;
The song and the silence in the heart,
That in part are prophecies, and in part
    Are longings wild and vain.
        And the voice of that fitful song
        Sings on, and is never still:
        'A boy's will is the wind's will,
And the thoughts of youth are long, long thoughts.'

There are things of which I may not speak:
    There are dreams that cannot die;
There are thoughts that make the strong heart weak,
And bring a pallor into the cheek,
    And a mist before the eye,
        And the words of that fatal song
        Come over me like a chill:
        'A boy's will is the wind's will,
And the thoughts of youth are long, long thoughts.'

Strange to me now are the forms I meet
    When I visit the dear old town;
But the native air is pure and sweet,
And the trees that oe'rshadow each well-known street,
    As they balance up and down,
        Are singing the beautiful song,
        Are sighing and whispering still:
        'A boy's will is the wind's will,
And the thoughts of youth are long, long thoughts.'

I remember the bulwarks by the shore,
    And the fort upon the hill;
The sunrise gun, with its hollow roar,
The drum-beat repeated o'er and o'er,
    And the bugle wild and shrill.
        And the music of that old song
        Throbs in my memory still:
        'A boy's will is the wind's will,
And the thoughts of youth are long, long thoughts.'

I remember the sea-fight far away,
    How it thundered o'er the tide!
And the dead captains, as they lay
In their graves, o'erlooking the tranquil bay,
    Where they in battle died.
        And the sound of that mournful song
        Goes through me with a thrill:
        'A boy's will is the wind's will,
And the thoughts of youth are long, long thoughts.'

I can see the breezy dome of groves,
    The shadows of Deering's Woods;
And the friendships old and the early loves
Come back with a sabbath sound, as of doves
    In quiet neighborhoods.
        And the verse of that sweet old song,
        It flutters and murmurs still:
        'A boy's will is the wind's will,
And the thoughts of youth are long, long thoughts.'

And Deering's Woods are fresh and fair,
   And with joy that is almost pain
My heart goes back to wander there,
And among the dreams of the days that were,
   I find my lost youth again.
     And the strange and beautiful song,
     The groves are repeating it still:
     'A boy's will is the wind's will,
And the thoughts of youth are long, long thoughts.'

HENRY WADSWORTH LONGFELLOW

the beautiful town: Portland, Maine

SAINT APOLLINARE IN CLASSE

This is God's hive; the bees
of Hybla never stored
ripe honey, such as these
rich walls afford.

Thought swarmed here once; the stark
Thebaid brake its comb,
and poured out of the dark
wild honey to Rome.

Then, as of old,
the skies of Patmos dipt:
very gold of very gold
glowed in the crypt,

and flawless, lit with green
cool light as from a wave,
the sea-veined cipolline
pillared the nave.

What sweetness ventured thus
to tempt Theology
to build her such a house?
or set the daring bee

so wide to rove, that men
have never wholly lost
the gold that clustered then
about the Host?

R. N. D. WILSON

Saint Apollinare in Classe: an
   early Christian
   basilica, Ravenna

≽ ≼

A CRY

March is returning to that wonder-shore
the swallows! for the wood at last is green;
and the wind brings them, the wind scatters them,
but each one finds its own belovèd nest.

Ah, blessèd is that child, the child who breathes
the essence of the orange, of the quince;
that child who, lost, all lost in his young dream,
looks, and does not perceive what his eyes see.

His mother calls him, offers him some bread,
fresh bread she hands him, but he does not care;
he takes it, nibbles . . . life is safe, so he
lives not today—he lives the splendid morrow.

Those days go by! and comes the real today:
and the bad times, the unfriendly times, are here;
comes hunger, comes exile, comes the long toil,
and only in a dream an old man goes back home.

In a dream he revisits that dear nest—
he has become a swallow! he can fly!
he is flying! and oh, how glad he is;
and the joy wakes him, and he cries a cry.

And every one of you knows of what nest
I speak, in tears! knows what land that is,
knows what a sorrow this my verse unfolds;
and one of you shall know I do not laugh.

FRANCESCO BIANCO

what land that is: Italy

PASTORAL

I, who have ridden the world
    From day's end to day's end,
Am fallen on fields and meadows
    Where shepherds tend

Slow-moving flocks; the air
    Is hot and still,
Sheep nuzzle the stream
    Drinking their fill.

The hours bring evening on:
    Dogs nip and bark,
The sheep are folded safe
    Well before dark.

High overhead the clouds
    Still gleam with gold,
The ever-wandering flock
    No shepherds fold.

WILLARD TRASK

⊰ *NOTES* ⊱

William Dunbar's "In Honour of the City of London" could not be modernized even to the extent that his earlier poem was (see Section 7). But a poet's view of London around 1500, and a Scots poet to boot, who saw the English metropolis with fresh eyes, cannot be altogether omitted, and I give three of its stanzas here:

London, thou art of townes *A per se,*
  Soveraign of cities, seemliest in sight,
Of high renoun, riches and royaltie,
    Of lordis, barons, and many a goodly knyght;
    Of most delectable lusty ladies bright;
Of famous prelatis, in habitis clericall;
    Of merchauntis full of substaunce and of myght:
London, thou art the flour of Cities all.

       . . .

Above all ryvers thy Ryver hath renowne,
  Whose beryall stremys, pleasaunt and preclare,
Under thy lusty wallys renneth down,
    Where many a swan doth swymme with wyngis fair;
    Where many a barge doth saile and row with are;
Where many a ship doth rest with top-royall.
    O, towne of townes! patrone and not compare,
London, thou art the flour of Cities all.

       . . .

Strong be thy wallis that about thee standis;
  Wise be the people that within thee dwellis;
Fresh is thy ryver with his lusty strandis;
    Blith be thy chirches, wele sownyng be thy bellis;
    Rich be thy merchauntis in substaunce that excellis;
Fair be their wives, right lovesom, white and small;
    Clere be thy virgyns, lusty under kellis:
London, thou art the flour of Cities all.

Wordsworth's sonnet was written in 1802, five years after Napoleon conquered Venice, an independent republic since the ninth century. The annual ceremony of espousing the sea originated in 1177, when the Venetians defeated the Germans in a naval battle and Pope Alexander III gave the Doge a ring with which to wed the Adriatic as a sign of dominion. In 1815, Shelley addressed a sonnet to Wordsworth modeled on the earlier one:

Poet of Nature, thou hast wept to know
That things depart which never may return:
Childhood and youth, friendship and love's first glow,
Have fled like sweet dreams, leaving thee to mourn.
These common woes I feel. One loss is mine
Which thou too feel'st, yet I alone deplore.
Thou wert as a lone star, whose light did shine
On some frail bark in winter's midnight roar:
Thou hast like to a rock-built refuge stood
Above the blind and battling multitude:
In honored poverty thy voice did weave
Songs consecrate to truth and liberty—
Deserting these, thou leavest me to grieve,
Thus having been, that thou shouldst cease to be.

John Hall Wheelock's famous "Sunday Evening in the Common" appeared in *The Harvard Monthly* a decade or so before E. E. Cummings became a contributor, and editor, of that undergraduate publication. The following account of the poem's genesis was written for this book by Mr. Wheelock:

"During the spring of our freshman year at college, Van Wyck Brooks and I had formed the habit of dining in Boston on Sunday evenings. After dinner, weather permitting, we would stroll in the Boston Common, descanting on the great themes of art and song, and discussing world problems, some of which, I seem to remember, we settled then and there. These pleasant occasions continued into June, and that summer, while at the seashore, I wrote a poem in celebration of one of them, under the title 'Sunday Evening in the Common.'

"In October of that year—1905, to be exact—on my return to college, I submitted the poem to *The Harvard Monthly*. Before doing so, however, I felt I must find a substitute for the name 'Van Wyck,' in line one of stanza three. I was shy about using the name of my friend—too shy, in fact, to show him the poem—and I felt he might not like to have his name appear in a published poem, should *The Harvard Monthly* decide to take it. The substitute given name must be a two-syllable name, and one that none of my friends was called by. Preferably, it should be iambic, with the stress on the second syllable, as in 'Van Wyck.' The name 'Edwin' satisfied the first requirement, and since I was unable to think of any two-syllable name with the stress on the second syllable, I settled for 'Edwin' as substitute, though it altered, being trochaic, the cadence of the line and, or so I thought, for the worse. *The Harvard Monthly* accepted the poem, and it appeared at some time in 1906, I believe [June, 1907]. Later, when the poem was included in my first book, *The Human Fantasy,* I restored the original 'Van Wyck.'

"In 1961, fifty-five years after its first publication, at a dinner given by The American Academy of Arts and Letters to honor Van Wyck Brooks, on the occasion of his seventy-fifth birthday, I had the pleasure of reading the poem to him and to the assemblage."

There is an echo from Mr. Wheelock's second stanza in the second part of T. S. Eliot's "Portrait of a Lady":

> Except when a street piano, mechanical and tired
> Reiterates some worn-out common song
> With the smell of hyacinths across the garden. . . .

Longfellow grew up in Portland—formerly Falmouth—in the District of Maine, and the incidents recorded in "My Lost Youth" depict the seaport town of his boyhood. In Casco Bay, Portland's harbor, loomed the "islands that were the Hesperides." During the War of 1812, the inhabitants heard the guns in the sea battle between the British and American brigs—the *Boxer* and the *Enterprise*—and Longfellow himself saw the bodies of the two captains brought ashore and buried with military honors on the hill overlooking the bay. Deering's Woods were a grove of oaks on the outskirts of the town.

I am once more indebted to my friend Willard Trask, this time for the Lapland song quoted by Longfellow in his poem, from which Robert Frost got the title of his first book. The song was originally published in Lappish, together with a Latin translation, in Johannes Scheffer's *Lapponia,* Frankfurt, 1673. Longfellow probably saw it in the German translation from Scheffer's Latin in Johann Gottfried von Herder's *Stimmen der Völker in Liedern* ("Voices of the Peoples in Songs"), Upsala, 1815. Mr. Trask's translation from the German follows:

JOURNEYING TO HIS SWEETHEART

> Sun! cast your brightest rays on Orra Lake!
> I would climb to the top of every fir
> If only I knew I would see Orra Lake.

> I would climb it and look toward my sweetheart
> Where she is now among flowers.

I would cut off its twigs, its young fresh twigs,
All its little branches I would cut off, its little green branches.

If I had wings to fly to you, crows' wings,
I would follow the course of the clouds as they drift toward Orra Lake.

But I have no wings, ducks' wings,
Nor feet, the swimming feet of geese, to take me to you.

Long enough have you waited, so many days,
Your loveliest days,
With your sweet eyes and your fond heart.

And if you tried to flee far away from me,
I would quickly catch you.

What is stronger and more binding than iron chains, than braided hair?
So love binds our feelings
And changes will and thought.

A boy's will is the wind's will,
The thoughts of youth are long thoughts.

If I listened to them all,
I would stray from the road, the right road.

I have a resolve, I will obey it,
Then I know I shall find the right road.

Mr. Trask, well known as a translator, is the author of *Joan of Arc: A Self-Portrait,* and a poet whose work wears a classic grace. A literary portrait of him appeared in *The Literary Review,* Vol. I, No. 2, under the title "Willard R. Trask: A Universal Garland," the latter being made up of his translations from medieval French and Latin, Portuguese, Italian, German, and, with a collaborator, Chinese.

12.

Seasons

12. SEASONS

PIED BEAUTY

Glory be to God for dappled things—
    For skies of couple-color as a brinded cow;
        For rose-moles all in stipple upon trout that swim;
Fresh-firecoal chestnut-falls; finches' wings;
    Landscape plotted and pieced—fold, fallow, and plough;
        And áll trádes, their gear and tackle and trim.

All things counter, original, spare, strange;
    Whatever is fickle, freckled (who knows how?)
        With swift, slow; sweet, sour; adazzle, dim;
He fathers-forth whose beauty is past change:
            Praise him.

GERARD MANLEY HOPKINS

SONG

    Hark! hark! the lark at heaven's gate sings,
        And Phoebus 'gins arise,
    His steeds to water at those springs
        On chaliced flowers that lies;
    And winking Mary-buds begin
        To ope their golden eyes:
    With every thing that pretty is,
        My lady sweet, arise:
          Arise, arise!

WILLIAM SHAKESPEARE

FAIR IS MY LOVE, FOR APRIL IN HER FACE

Fair is my love, for April in her face;
  Her lovely breasts September claims his part;
And lordly July in her eyes takes place;
  But cold December dwelleth in her heart:
Blest be the months that set my thoughts on fire!
Accurst that month that hind'reth my desire!

Like Phoebus' fire, so sparkle both her eyes;
  As air perfumed with amber is her breath;
Like swelling waves her lovely teats do rise;
  As earth her heart, cold, dateth me to death:
Ay me, poor man, that on the earth do live,
When unkind earth death and despair doth give!

In pomp sits mercy seated in her face;
  Love 'twixt her breasts his trophies doth imprint;
Her eyes shine favor, courtesy, and grace;
  But touch her heart, ah, that is framed of flint!
That 'fore my harvest in the grass bears grain,
The rock will wear, washed with a winter's rain.

                                        ROBERT GREENE

THE INWARD MORNING

Packed in my mind lie all the clothes
  Which outward nature wears,
And in its fashion's hourly change
  It all things else repairs.

In vain I look for change abroad,
  And can no difference find,
Till some new ray of peace uncalled
  Illumes my inmost mind.

What is it gilds the trees and clouds,
  And paints the heavens so gay,
But yonder fast-abiding light
  With its unchanging ray?

Lo, when the sun streams through the wood,
  Upon a winter's morn,
Where'er his silent beams intrude
  The murky night is gone.

How could the patient pine have known
  The morning breeze would come,
Or humble flowers anticipate
  The insect's noonday hum—

Till the new light with morning cheer
  From far streamed through the aisles,
And nimbly told the forest trees
  For many stretching miles?

I've heard within my inmost soul
  Such cheerful morning news,
In the horizon of my mind
  Have seen such orient hues,

As in the twilight of the dawn,
  When the first birds awake,
Are heard within some silent wood,
  Where they the small twigs break,

Or in the eastern skies are seen,
  Before the sun appears,
The harbingers of summer heats
  Which from afar he bears.

HENRY DAVID THOREAU

M. ANTONIO FLAMINIO:
TO HIS FARM

Cool shades, air-fanning groves,
With your soft whisperings,
Where pleasure smiling roves
Through dewy caves and springs,
And bathes her purple wings:

With flowers-enamel'd ground,
(Nature's fair tapestry),
Where chattering birds abound,
Flick'ring from tree to tree
With change of melody:

Sweet liberty and leisures,
Where still the Muses keep,
O! if to those true treasures
That from your bosom peep,
I might securely creep:

If I might spend my days
(Remote from public brawls),
Now tuning lovely lays,
Now lightfoot madrigals,
Ne'er check'd with sudden calls:

Now follow sleep that goes
Rustling i' th' greenwood shade;
Now milk my goat, that knows,
(With her young, fearful cade),
The pail i' th' cooly glade:

And with bowls fill'd to th' brims
Of milky moisture new,
To water my dried limbs,
And t' all the wrangling crew
Of cares to bid adieu:

What life then should I lead!
How like then would it be
Unto the gods, that tread
I' th' starry gallery
Of true felicity!

But you, O virgins sweet,
In Helicon that dwell,
That oft the fountains greet,
When you the pleasures tell
I' th' country that excel:

If my life, though dear,
For your far dearer sake,
To yield would nothing fear,
From city's tumults take me
And free i' th' country make me.

JOHN ASHMORE

cade: young one, cadet
Helicon: the mountain sacred to the
   Muses

☙ ❧

THE APOLOGY

Think me not unkind and rude
   That I walk alone in grove and glen;
I go to the god of the wood
   To fetch his word to men.

Tax not my sloth that I
   Fold my arms beside the brook;
Each cloud that floated in the sky
   Writes a letter in my book.

Chide me not, laborious band,
    For the idle flowers I brought;
Every aster in my hand
    Goes home loaded with a thought.

There was never mystery
    But 'tis figured in the flowers;
Was never secret history
    But birds tell it in the bowers.

One harvest from thy field
    Homeward brought the oxen strong;
A second crop thine acres yield,
    Which I gather in a song.

            RALPH WALDO EMERSON

THE SPRING

Though you be absent here, I needs must say
The trees as beauteous are, and flowers as gay,
    As ever they were wont to be;
    Nay the birds' rural music too
    Is as melodious and free,
    As if they sung to pleasure you:
I saw a rose-bud ope this morn; I'll swear
The blushing morning opened not more fair.

How could it be so fair, and you away?
How could the trees be beauteous, flowers so gay?
    Could they remember but last year,
    How you did them, they you delight,
    The sprouting leaves which saw you here,
    And called their fellows to the sight,
Would, looking round for the same sight in vain,
Creep back into their silent barks again.

Where'er you walked trees were as reverent made,
As when of old gods dwelt in every shade.

Is 't possible they should not know,
What loss of honor they sustain,
   That thus they smile and flourish now,
   And still their former pride retain?
Dull creatures! 'tis not without cause that she,
Who fled the god of wit, was made a tree.

In ancient times sure they much wiser were,
When they rejoiced the Thracian verse to hear;
   In vain did nature bid them stay,
   When Orpheus had his song begun,
   They called their wondering roots away,
   And bade them silent to him run.
How would those learned trees have followed you?
You would have drawn them, and their poet, too.

But who can blame them now? for, since you're gone,
They're here the only fair, and shine alone.
   You did their natural rights invade;
   Wherever you did walk or sit,
   The thickest boughs could make no shade,
   Although the sun had granted it:
The fairest flowers could please no more, near you,
Than painted flowers, set next to them, could do.

Whene'er then you come hither, that shall be
The time, which this to others is, to me.
   The little joys which here are now,
   The name of punishments do bear,
   When by their sight they let us know
   How we deprived of greater are.
'Tis you the best of seasons with you bring;
This is for beasts, and that for men the spring.

                    ABRAHAM COWLEY

she: Daphne
god of wit: Apollo
the only fair: the only fair ones, with a play on ladies

CORINNA'S GOING A-MAYING

Get up, get up for shame! the blooming morn
Upon her wings presents the god unshorn.
   See how Aurora throws her fair
   Fresh-quilted colors through the air:
   Get up, sweet slug-a-bed, and see
   The dew-bespangling herb and tree.
Each flower has wept, and bow'd toward the east,
Above an hour since; yet you not drest,
   Nay! not so much as out of bed?
   When all the birds have matins said,
   And sung their thankful hymns: 'tis sin,
   Nay, profanation, to keep in,—
Whenas a thousand virgins on this day,
Spring, sooner than the lark, to fetch in May.

Rise; and put on your foliage, and be seen
To come forth, like the springtime, fresh and green,
   And sweet as Flora. Take no care
   For jewels for your gown, or hair:
   Fear not; the leaves will strew
   Gems in abundance upon you:
Besides, the childhood of the day has kept,
Against you come, some orient pearls unwept:
   Come, and receive them while the light
   Hangs on the dew-locks of the night:
   And Titan on the eastern hill
   Retires himself, or else stands still
Till you come forth. Wash, dress, be brief in praying;
Few beads are best, when once we go a-Maying.

Come, my Corinna, come; and coming, mark
How each field turns a street; each street a park
   Made green, and trimm'd with trees: see how
   Devotion gives each house a bough
   Or branch: each porch, each door, ere this,

An ark, a tabernacle is
Made up of white-thorn neatly interwove;
As if here were those cooler shades of love.
    Can such delights be in the street,
    And open fields, and we not see 't?
    Come, we'll abroad: and let's obey
    The proclamation made for May:
And sin no more, as we have done, by staying;
But, my Corinna, come, let's go a-Maying.

There's not a budding boy, or girl, this day,
But is got up, and gone to bring in May.
    A deal of youth, ere this, is come
    Back, and with white-thorn laden home.
    Some have dispatch'd their cakes and cream,
    Before that we have left to dream:
And some have wept, and woo'd, and plighted troth,
And chose their priest, ere we can cast off sloth:
    Many a green gown has been given;
    Many a kiss, both odd and even:
    Many a glance, too, has been sent
    From out the eye, love's firmament:
Many a jest told of the keys betraying
This night, and locks pick'd:—yet we're not a-Maying.

—Come, let us go, while we are in our prime;
And take the harmless folly of the time!
    We shall grow old apace, and die
    Before we know our liberty.
    Our life is short; and our days run
    As fast away as does the sun:—
And as a vapor, or a drop of rain
Once lost, can ne'er be found again:
    So when or you or I are made
    A fable, song, or fleeting shade,
    All love, all liking, all delight
    Lies drown'd with us in endless night.

—Then while time serves, and we are but decaying,
Come, my Corinna! come, let's go a-Maying.

ROBERT HERRICK

Titan: here, the sun god
green gown: rolling in the grass

※ ※

TO AUTUMN

O Autumn, laden with fruit, and stainèd
With the blood of the grape, pass not, but sit
Beneath my shady roof; there thou may'st rest
And tune thy jolly voice to my fresh pipe,
And all the daughters of the year shall dance!
Sing now the lusty song of fruits and flowers.

'The narrow bud opens her beauties to
The sun, and love runs in her thrilling veins;
Blossoms hang round the brows of Morning, and
Flourish down the bright cheek of modest Eve,
Till clust'ring Summer breaks forth into singing,
And feather'd clouds strew flowers round her head.

'The spirits of the air live on the smells
Of fruit; and Joy, with pinions light, roves round
The gardens, or sits singing in the trees.'
Thus sang the jolly Autumn as he sat;
Then rose, girded himself, and o'er the bleak
Hills fled from our sight; but left his golden load.

WILLIAM BLAKE

pipe: musical wind-instrument

※ ※

OCTOBER

Now, every day, the runner sun applies
To shorter courses for a lesser prize.

He, to whom all was possible, is proud
If he can only shoulder back a cloud.

This morning I was up to see him rise,
Stared in his face and never blinked my eyes.

Was this the light no vision could endure,
This filtered water, tasteless, cold and pure?

It trickled down the sky and touched the leaves;
They let it fall like gently dripping eaves.

I could imagine it among the hills;
It wandered down their sides in little rills.

Through grassy meadows I could trace its road,
Lost it in stubble where the fields were mowed.

I saw it find the river, tumble in.
But where did water end and light begin?

The streams I followed seemed to change their course:
They flowed again, but what had been their source

Was now their ocean. My distracted eye
Saw river-water spreading through the sky.

This is the nipping time of feasts and fairs,
Markets enchanted by the smell of pears:

An active time for him who acts; for him
Who looks, a time in which the world grows dim,

A heavy time, a time in which to brood:
Silver to bronze—more precious, more subdued.

WILLARD TRASK

MY NOVEMBER GUEST

My Sorrow, when she's here with me,
　　Thinks these dark days of autumn rain
Are beautiful as days can be;
She loves the bare, the withered tree;
　　She walks the sodden pasture lane.

Her pleasure will not let me stay.
　　She talks and I am fain to list:
She's glad the birds are gone away,
She's glad her simple worsted grey
　　Is silver now with clinging mist.

The desolate, deserted trees,
　　The faded earth, the heavy sky,
The beauties she so truly sees,
She thinks I have no eye for these,
　　And vexes me for reason why.

Not yesterday I learned to know
　　The love of bare November days
Before the coming of the snow,
But it were vain to tell her so,
　　And they are better for her praise.

ROBERT FROST

❧ ❦

WINTER

Now winter nights enlarge
The number of their hours,
And clouds their storms discharge
Upon the airy towers.

Let now the chimneys blaze,
And cups o'erflow with wine;
Let well-tuned words amaze
With harmony divine.
Now yellow waxen lights
Shall wait on honey love,
While youthful revels, masques, and courtly sights
Sleep's leaden spells remove.

This time doth well dispense
With lovers' long discourse;
Much speech hath some defence,
Though beauty no remorse.
All do not all things well;
Some measures comely tread,
Some knotted riddles tell,
Some poems smoothly read.
The summer hath its joys
And winter his delights;
Though love and all his pleasures are but toys,
They shorten tedious nights.

THOMAS CAMPION

THE OXEN

Christmas Eve, and twelve of the clock.
   'Now they are all on their knees,'
An elder said as we sat in a flock
   By the elders in hearthside ease.

We pictured the meek mild creatures where
   They dwelt in their strawy pen,
Nor did it occur to one of us there
   To doubt they were kneeling then.

So fair a fancy few would weave
  In these years! Yet, I feel,
If someone said on Christmas Eve,
  'Come; see the oxen kneel,

'In the lonely barton by yonder coomb
  Our childhood used to know,'
I should go with him in the gloom,
  Hoping it might be so.

THOMAS HARDY

barton: farmyard
coomb: little valley

⋈ *NOTES* ⋈

Robert Greene's sensual lyric is from *Perimedes the Blacksmith,* 1588, which is also notable for an attack on Marlowe, and perhaps on Shakespeare as well: "Lately two gentlemen poets made two madmen of Rome beat it out of their paper bucklers and had it in derision for that I could not make my verses jet upon the stage in tragical buskins, every word filling the mouth like the fa-burden of Bow-bell, daring God out of heaven with that atheist Tamburlaine." Greene was obviously referring to the prologue of Marlowe's sensational play:

> From jigging veins of rhyming mother wits,
> And such conceits as clownage keeps in pay,
> We'll lead you to the stately tent of War,
> Where you shall hear the Scythian Tamburlaine
> Threat'ning the world with high astounding terms.

It is also possible he was referring to *Titus Andronicus,* which, as I have suggested elsewhere, may have been an early collaboration between Marlowe and Shakespeare. More curious is the following verse from Thomas Morley's *Madrigals to Four Voices,* 1594:

> April is in my mistress' face,
> And July in her eyes hath place;
> Within her bosom is September,
> But in her heart a cold December.

M. Antonio Flaminio was a Renaissance Italian who wrote in Latin. John Ashmore, who translated Flaminio's "To His Farm," published *Certain Odes of Horace,* Englished in 1621, and that is about all that is known of him (Marshall, *Rare Poems of the Seventeenth Century,* p. 3). Another interesting example of the word "cade," which occurs in Ashmore's fifth stanza, is given by Marshall on p. 222: a certain Jane Lovet, in her 1551 will, bequeathed "Three Cade lambes that go abowte the house."

No doubt a great impetus to country longings was given English poets by the translations of bucolic themes, such as Ashmore's. But disappointments in town also inspired them, expressed by Abraham Cowley in "The Wish" as follows:

> Well then; I now do plainly see
> This busy world and I shall ne'er agree.

The very honey of all earthly joy
Does, of all meats, the soonest cloy;
  And they, methinks, deserve my pity
Who for it can endure the stings,
 The crowd, and buzz, and murmurings
  Of this great hive, the city.

And yet, ere I descend to the grave,
May I a small house and large garden have;
And a few friends, and many books, both true,
Both wise, and both delightful, too!

On this, Dr. Johnson commented: "By the lovers of virtue and of wit it will be solicitously asked, if he now was happy. Let them peruse one of his letters accidentally preserved by Peck, which I recommend to the consideration of all that may hereafter pant for solitude:

To Dr. Thomas Sprat.
Chertsey, May 21, 1665.
 The first night that I came hither I caught so great a cold, with a defluxion of rheum, as made me keep my chamber ten days. And, two after, had such a bruise on my ribs with a fall, that I am yet unable to move or turn myself in bed. This is my personal fortune here to begin with. And, besides, I can get no money from my tenants, and have my meadows eaten up every night by cattle put in by my neighbors. What this signifies, or may come to in time, God knows; if it be ominous, it can end in nothing less than hanging. Another misfortune has been, and stranger than all the rest, that you have broke your word with me, and failed to come, even though you told Mr. Bois that you would.

He did not long enjoy the pleasure or suffer the uneasiness of solitude; for he died at the Porch-house in Chertsey, in 1667, in the 49th year of his age." Johnson, to be sure, hated the country, and told Boswell: "Sir, when a man is tired of London, he is tired of life."

Thomas Hardy's "Afterwards" sums up all we can wish for in a poet writing about the country, and I therefore give it here, to crown the seasons and this book:

When the Present has latched its postern behind my tremulous stay,
  And the May month flaps its glad green leaves like wings,
Delicate-filmed as a new-spun silk, will the neighbors say,
  'He was a man who used to notice such things'?

If it be in the dusk when, like an eyelid's soundless blink,
  The dewfall-hawk comes crossing the shades to alight
Upon the wind-warped upland thorn, a gazer may think,
  'To him this must have been a familiar sight.'

If I pass during some nocturnal blackness, mothy and warm,
  When the hedgehog travels furtively over the lawn,
One may say, 'He strove that such innocent creatures should
    come to no harm,
  But he could do little for them; and now he is gone.'

If, when hearing that I have been stilled at last, they stand at the door,
  Watching the full-starred heavens that winter sees,
Will this thought rise on those who will meet my face no more,
  'He was one who had an eye for such mysteries'?

And will any say when my bell of quittance is heard
    in the gloom,
  And a crossing breeze cuts a pause in its outrollings,
Till they rise again, as they were a new bell's boom,
  'He hears it not now, but used to notice such things'?

INDEX OF FIRST LINES

INDEX OF POETS